Travel Publications

KU-350-838

Orlando

must
SEES

Chief Editor	Cynthia Clayton Ochterbeck
Senior Editor	M. Linda Lee
Writers	Diane Bair and Pamela Wright, Bair-Wright Associates
Production Coordinator	Allison M. Simpson
Cartography	Peter Wrenn
Photo Editor	Brigitta L. House
Documentation	Doug Rogers, Martha Hunt
Proofreader	Margo Browning
Production	Octavo Design and Production, Inc. Apopka, Florida
Cover Design	Paris Venise Design Paris, 17e
Printing and Binding	Quebecor World Laval, Québec

Travel Publications

Michelin North America
One Parkway South
Greenville, SC 29615
USA
800-423-0485
www.michelin-us.com
email: TheGreenGuide@us.michelin.com

Special Sales:

For information regarding bulk sales, customized editions and premium sales, please contact our Customer Service Departments:

USA – 800-423-0485   **Canada** – 800-361-8236

Manufacture française des pneumatiques Michelin

Société en commandite par actions au capital de 304 000 000 EUR
Place des Carmes-Déchaux — 63 Clermont-Ferrand (France)
R.C.S. Clermont-FD B 855 800 507

Note to the reader:

While every effort is made to ensure that all information in this guide is correct and up-to-date, Michelin Travel Publications (Michelin North America, Inc.) accepts no liability for any direct, indirect or consequential losses howsoever caused so far as such can be excluded by law.

Admission prices listed for sights in this guide are for a single adult, unless otherwise specified.

Welcome To Orlando

Main Street U.S.A. at Disney's Magic Kingdom

Table of Contents

Table of Contents

THE MICHELIN STARS

For more than 75 years, travelers have used the Michelin stars to take the guesswork out of planning a trip. Our star-rating system helps you make the best decision on where to go, what to do, and what to see. A three-star rating means it's one of the "absolutelys"; two stars means it's one of the "should sees"; and one star says it's one of the "sees" —a must if you have the time.

★★★ Absolutely Must See
★★ Really Must See
★ Must See

Three-Star Sights ★★★

Busch Gardens Tampa Bay ★★★
Castillo de San Marcos National Monument ★★★
Disney MGM Studios ★★★
Disney's Animal Kingdom ★★★
Epcot ★★★
Kennedy Space Center ★★★
Magic Kingdom ★★★
Salvador Dalí Museum ★★★
SeaWorld Orlando ★★★
St. Augustine ★★★
Universal Orlando ★★★
Universal's Islands of Adventure ★★★

Two-Star Sights ★★

Cathedral-Basilica of St. Augustine ★★
Discovery Cove ★★
Flagler College ★★
Gonzalez-Alvarez House ★★
Historic Bok Sanctuary ★★
Lightner Museum ★★

Two-Star Sights★★

Merritt Island National Wildlife Refuge★★
Museum of Science & Industry★★
Ocala National Forest★★
Playalinda Beach★★
St. Augustine Alligator Farm★★
St. Petersburg★★
Tampa★★
Ximenez-Fatio House★★
Ybor City★★

One-Star Sights★

Charles Hosmer Morse Museum of American Art★
Crystal River★
Florida Aquarium★
Gatorland★
Government House Museum★
Harry P. Leu Gardens★
Marineland★
Mission de Nombre de Dios★
Museum of Fine Arts★
Ocala★
Old St. Augustine Village★
Orange Avenue★
Orange County Regional History Center★
Orlando Museum of Art★
Orlando Science Center★
The Pier★
Silver Springs★
Spanish Quarter Village★
Tarpon Springs★

Calendar Of Events

Listed below is a selection of Orlando's most popular annual events. Please note that dates may vary
from year to year. For more detailed information,
contact Orlando's Official Visitor Center
(407-363-5872; www.orlandoinfo.com).

January

Florida Citrus Bowl   407-423-2476
Citrus Bowl   www.fcsports.com
Orlando Museum of Art Annual Wine and Art Event
Orlando Museum of Art   407-824-4321
                                   www.omart.org
Surf & Skate   407-224-2690
Universal CityWalk   www.citywalkorlando.com

February

Atlanta Braves spring training   407-824-4321
Disney's Wide World of Sports   www.disneysports.com
Black Heritage Celebration   407-824-4321
Epcot   www.disneyworld.com
Mardi Gras at Downtown Disney   407-934-7781
Pleasure Island   www.downtowndisney.com
Mardi Gras at Universal   407-363-8000
Universal Studios Florida   www.universalorlando.com
Silver Spurs Rodeo *(also Oct)*   407-847-4052
Silver Springs Rodeo Arena   www.silverspursrodeo.com

March

Central Florida Fair   407-295-3247
Central Florida Fairgrounds   www.centralfloridafair.com
Florida Film Festival   407-629-8587
Various locations   www.floridafilmfestival.com
Houston Astros Spring Training   407-933-5400
Osceola County Stadium,
    Kissimmee   www.astros.mlb.com
Kissimmee Bluegrass Festival   813-935-1561
Silver Springs Rodeo Arena   www.floridakiss.com

April

Spring Fiesta in the Park   407-246-2827
Robinson St. & Eola Dr., Lake Eola

May

Annual Cinco de Mayo Festival   407-224-WALK
Universal CityWalk   www.citywalkorlando.com
Epcot International
    Flower & Garden Festival   407-824-4321
Epcot   www.disneyworld.com
Star Wars Weekends   407-824-4321
Disney-MGM Studios   www.disneyworld.com

June

Annual Latin Culture Fiesta San Juan   407-351-1800
Wet 'n' Wild   www.wetnwild.com
Florida Film Festival   407-629-1088
Enzian Theater

July

Fourth of July at Disney World   407-824-4321
Various Disney parks   www.disneyworld.com
Lake Eola Picnic in the Park   407-246-2827
Independence Day Celebration, Lake Eola

August

Tampa Bay Buccaneers NFL Training Camp 407-839-3900
Disney Wide World   www.disneysports.com
   of Sports Complex

September

Annual Mexican Fiesta   407-420-6896
Downtown Orlando   www.downtownorlando.com
Rock the Universe   407-224-5500
Universal Studios Florida   www.universalorlando.com
Viva La Musica (Hispanic Heritage fiestas)407-363-2259
SeaWorld Orlando   www.seaworld.com

October

**Epcot's International
   Food & Wine Festival**   407-824-4321
Epcot   www.disneyworld.com
Halloween Horror Nights   407-224-5500
Universal Studios Florida   www.universalorlando.com
Mickey's Not-So-Scary Halloween Party 407-824-4321
Magic Kingdom   www.disneyworld.com
Shamu's Halloween Spooktacular   407-363-2259
SeaWorld Orlando   www.seaworld.com

November

Holidays Around the World   407-824-4321
Epcot World Showcase   www.disneyworld.com
Orlando Magic season opener   407-896-2442
T.D. Waterhouse Center   www.nba.com

December

Grand Masque New Year's Eve Ball   407-426-1739
Gaylord Palms Resort   www.grandemasque.org
Holidays in the City   407-934-7781
Downtown Disney   www.downtowndisney.com
Mickey's Very Merry Christmas Party   407-824-4321
Magic Kingdom   www.disneyworld.com

Must Know: Practical Information

Area Code: 407

VISITOR INFORMATION

Before you go, check with the following organizations to obtain a visitor's guide, maps and information on accommodations, dining, shopping, entertainment, festivals and recreation:

Orlando/Orange County Convention and Visitors Bureau

> 6700 Forum Dr., Suite 100,
> Orlando, FL 32821
> 363-5800; www.orlandoinfo.com

Official Visitor Center

> 8723 International Dr., Suite 101,
> Orlando, FL 32819
> 363-5872; www.orlandoinfo.com
> Open year-round daily 8am–7pm

Kissimmee-St. Cloud Convention and Visitors Bureau

> 1925 E. Highway 192, Kissimmee, FL 34742
> 847-5000 or 800-333-5477
> www.floridakiss.com

Orlando Magicard – Offers the holder savings on accommodations, attractions, dining and shopping *(free; for information, call 800-551-0181).*

WHEN TO GO

Theme parks are busiest during summer, Christmas and spring holidays. The least crowded period falls between Thanksgiving and December 25, followed by September and October, then January. Sunday morning tends to be the least crowded time at all the parks. During the summer months *(May–Sept)* humidity is high and afternoon thundershowers are frequent. Bring lightweight, comfortable clothing, a hat and sunscreen.

Tips for Special Visitors

Disabled Travelers – Federal law requires that businesses (including hotels and restaurants) provide access for the disabled, devices for the hearing impaired and designated parking spaces. For further information, contact the Society for Accessible Travel and Hospitality (SATH), 347 Fifth Ave., Suite 610, New York, NY 10016 *(212-447-7284; www.sath.org).*

All national parks have facilities for the disabled, and offer free or discounted passes. For details, contact the National Park Service *(Office of Public Inquiries, P.O. Box 37127, Room 1013, Washington, DC 20013-7127; 202-208-4747; www.nps.gov).*

Passengers who will need assistance with train or bus travel should give advance notice to Amtrak *(800-872-7245 or 800-523-6590/TDD; www.amtrak.com)* or Greyhound *(800-752-4841 or 800-345-3109/TDD; www.greyhound.com).* To rent a hand-controlled car, make reservations in advance with the rental company.

Senior Citizens – Many hotels, attractions and restaurants offer discounts to visitors age 62 or older (proof of age may be required). The **American Association of Retired Persons** (AARP), *(601 E St. NW, Washington, DC 20049; 202-424-3410; www.aarp.com)* offers discounts to its members.

Average Seasonal Temperatures in Orlando

	Jan	Apr	July	Oct
Avg. High	61°F/16°C	72°F/22°C	83°F/29°C	74°F/23°C
Avg. Low	50°F/10°C	60°F/16°C	73°F/23°C	65°F/18°C

Hurricanes

The hurricane season usually lasts from June to November with the greatest activity generally occurring from August to October. Hurricanes begin as tropical depressions and are classified as hurricanes once the winds reach 74mph. The National Hurricane Center in Miami, Florida tracks all storms and issues advisories every six hours; stay tuned to radio and television. A hurricane **watch** is announced if hurricane conditions may threaten an area within 36 hours; a hurricane **warning** is issued if sustained winds of at least 74mph are expected within 24 hours.

Hurricane precautionary measures:
• Check your car battery and fill up the gas tank.
• Make sure you have a battery-operated radio and extra batteries.
• Collect plenty of fresh water in containers and bathtubs.
• When staying in coastal areas, familiarize yourself with evacuation routes.
• Stay indoors once the hurricane has struck.
• Be aware of storm surges in coastal regions.
• Never take a hurricane lightly, and follow instructions issued by local authorities.

GETTING THERE

By Air – Orlando International Airport (MCO) is located 7mi south of the city *(825-2001; www.state.fla.us/goaa)*. An information booth is located on Level 3, just beyond the food court *(open daily 7am–11pm; multilingual service; 825-2352)*. Transportation to International Drive and theme-park-area hotels is available via limo *($130)*; taxi *($25)*; and 24hr-shuttle vans *($14)* provided by Mears *(839-1570)*.

Lynx *(for schedules: 841-8240; www.golynx.com)* provides public bus service between S. Orange Ave. downtown and Orlando International Airport *(bus #11)*, and between the airport and International Drive *(bus #42)*. Hotel courtesy shuttles depart outside baggage claim on Level 1. Rental-car agencies are located in the airport parking garage.

Car Rental Company	Reservations	Web site
Alamo	800-327-9633	www.alamo.com
Avis	800-331-1212	www.avis.com
Budget	800-527-0700	www.drivebudget.com
Dollar	800-800-4000	www.dollar.com
Enterprise	800-325-8007	www.enterprise.com
Hertz	800-654-3131	www.hertz.com
National	800-227-7368	www.nationalcar.com
Thrifty	800-331-4200	www.thrifty.com

Must Know: Practical Information

By Train and Bus – Amtrak train stations are located at 1400 Sligh Blvd., Orlando; and at 150 W. Morse Blvd., Winter Park *(800-872-7245; www.amtrak.com)*. The Greyhound bus station is located at 555 N. John Young Pkwy. *(292-3424 or 800-231-2222; www.greyhound.com)*.

GETTING AROUND

By Public Transportation – Lynx provides local bus service *(year-round daily; $1.25; schedule & route information: 841-8240; www.golynx.com)*. Downtown **shuttle** service is provided by Lymo *(every 5min; 841-8240)*. I-Ride **trolley** system services the International Drive area *(daily 7am–midnight; every 15 minutes; 75¢ each way; 248-9590; www.iridetrolley.com)*.

By Car – The Beeline (Rte. 528), East-West Expressway and Central Florida GreeneWay are all toll roads. Metered downtown street parking costs 75¢/hr. The average rate for parking garages is $1/hr, $7/day. Parking information: 246-2154.

By Foot – Both the International Drive area (home to several restaurants, hotels and entertainment venues) and downtown Orlando's Orange Avenue, where nightclubs and bars are clustered, are well-lit and easily walkable.

FOREIGN VISITORS

In addition to the tourism offices throughout Florida, visitors from outside the US can obtain information in French, German, Japanese, Portuguese and Spanish from the web site of Visit Florida *(www.flausa.com)*, or from the US embassy or consulate in their country of residence. For a complete list of American consulates and embassies abroad, visit the Web site for the Department of State Bureau of Consular Affairs *(http://travel.state.gov/links.html)*.

Entry Requirements – Starting October 1, 2003, travelers entering the United States under the Visa Waiver Program (VWP) must have a machine-readable passport. Any traveler without a machine-readable passport will be required to obtain a visa before entering the US. Citizens of VWP countries are permitted to enter the US for general business or tourist purposes for a maximum of 90 days without needing a visa. Requirements for the Visa Waiver Program can be found at the Department of State's Visa Services Web site *(http://travel.state.gov/vwp.html)*.

All citizens of nonparticipating countries must have a visitor's visa. Upon entry, nonresident foreign visitors must present a valid passport and round-trip transportation ticket. Canadian citizens are not required to present a passport or visa, but they must present a valid picture ID and proof of citizenship. Naturalized Canadian citizens should carry their citizenship papers.

US Customs – All articles brought into the US must be declared at the time of entry. Prohibited items: plant material; firearms and ammunition (if not for sporting purposes); meat or poultry products. For information, contact the US Customs Service, 1300 Pennsylvania Ave. NW, Washington, DC 20229 *(202-354-1000; www.customs.gov)*.

Money and Currency Exchange – Visitors can exchange currency at downtown banks as well as at Orlando International Airport in the international terminal. Banks, stores, restaurants and hotels accept travelers' checks with picture identification. To report a lost or stolen credit card: American Express *(800-528-4800)*; Diners Club *(800-234-6377)*; MasterCard *(800-307-7309)*; or Visa *(800-336-8472)*.

Driving in the US – Visitors bearing valid driver's licenses issued by their country of residence are not required to obtain an International Driver's License. Drivers must carry vehicle registration and/or rental contract, and proof of automobile insurance at all times. Gasoline is sold by the gallon. Vehicles in the US are driven on the right-hand side of the road.

Electricity – Voltage in the US is 120 volts AC, 60 Hz. Foreign-made appliances may need AC adapters (available at specialty travel and electronics stores) and North American flat-blade plugs.

Taxes and Tipping – Prices displayed in the US do not include sales tax (6% in Florida), which is not reimbursable. It is customary to give a small gift of money—a **tip**—for services rendered to waiters (15–20% of bill), porters ($1 per bag), chambermaids ($1 per day) and cab drivers (15% of fare).

Measurement Equivalents

Degrees Fahrenheit	95°	86°	77°	68°	59°	50°	41°	32°	23°	14°
Degrees Celsius	35°	30°	25°	20°	15°	10°	5°	0°	-5°	-10°

1 inch = 2.54 centimeters   1 foot = 30.48 centimeters

1 mile = 1.609 kilometers   1 pound = 0.454 kilograms

1 quart = 0.946 liters   1 gallon = 3.785 liters

ACCOMMODATIONS
For a list of suggested accommodations, see Must Stay.

Be sure to make reservations three to five months in advance—especially for summer and holiday stays. Many hotels offer free shuttle service to Disney and Universal attractions.

Hotel Reservation Service – 800-950-0232. Central Reservation Service operates 24-hour courtesy phones at the airport *(339-4116)*.

Youth Hostel – Orlando/Kissimmee Resort *($14-$19/person; $30–$57/family; 396-8282)*.

Campgrounds and RV Parks – Two of the major ones are located on US-192 (also known as Irlo Bronson Hwy.) in Kissimmee: Raccoon Lake Camp Resort is located 4mi west of Walt Disney World *(8555 W. Irlo Bronson Hwy.; 239-4148 or 800-776-9644; www.raccoonlake.com)*; and Orlando-Kissimmee KOA Kampground *(4771 W. Irlo Bronson Hwy.; 396-2400 or 800-562-7791; www.koakampgrounds.com)*.

Must Know: Practical Information

Major hotel and motel chains with locations in Orlando include:

Property	Phone/Web site	Property	Phone/Web site
Best Western	800-528-1234 www.bestwestern.com	ITT Sheraton	800-325-3535 www.sheraton.com
Comfort, Clarion & Quality Inns	800-228-5150 www.comfortinn.com	Marriott	800-228-9290 www.marriott.com
Crowne Plaza	800-227-6963 www.crowneplaza.com	Omni	800-843-6664 www.omnihotels.com
Days Inn	800-325-2525 www.daysinn.com	Radisson	800-333-3333 www.radisson.com
Hilton	800-445-8667 www.hilton.com	Ramada	800-228-2828 www.ramada.com
Holiday Inn	800-465-4329 www.holiday-inn.com	Ritz-Carlton	800-241-3333 www.ritzcarlton.com
Howard Johnson	800-446-4656 www.hojo.com	Westin	800-848-0016 www.westin.com
Hyatt	800-233-1234 www.hyatt.com		

SPORTS AND RECREATION

Spectator Sports – Orlando Magic basketball (NBA), T.D. Waterhouse Centre *(896-2442; www.orlandomagic.com)*. Seminole Greyhound Park *(699-4510)*. Orlando-Seminole Jai Alai Fronton *(339-6221; www.orlandojaialai.com)*.

Golf – Many area golf clubs allow non-members. Captain's Choice Golf Services, Inc. books tee times and offers transportation to most local courses *(reservations: 352-1102; www.captainschoicegolf.com)*.
Public courses include International Golf Club *(239-6909)*; Casselberry *(699-9310)*; and Orange Lake Country Club *(239-0000)*.

> **Play Ball!**
> The Orlando area is also home to professional **baseball's spring training camps**. Warm-up practice starts in late February and "Grapefruit League" exhibition games are played daily through March. The Atlanta Braves play at Disney's Wide World of Sports *(939-1500; www.braves.mlb.com)*, while the Houston Astros train in Kissimmee, at Osceola County Stadium *(933-6500; www.astros.mlb.com)*.

DOING DISNEY

For general information and to request a free vacation guide, contact:

Walt Disney World Guest Information
P.O. Box 10040, Lake Buena Vista FL 32830-0040
824-4321; www.disneyworld.com

All Walt Disney World Resort attractions are accessible to visitors with disabilities. Proper dress is required at all times. Baby strollers and wheelchair rentals are available in limited quantities *($8)*.

Must Know: Practical Information

Visitor Services – For most visitor services (foreign language maps, information for guests with disabilities, baby facilities, lost and found, storage lockers, banking facilities, camera centers, Disney character greetings), contact **Guest Relations** at the individual parks:

- City Hall, Main Street U.S.A. at **Magic Kingdom**
- Near the gift stop at **Epcot**
- On Hollywood Boulevard at **Disney-MGM Studios**
- Next to Creature Comfort at **Disney's Animal Kingdom**

Lost Children – Check the lost children's logbooks at Baby Care Centers or contact Guest Relations.

Medical Emergencies – Contact the First Aid Centers near Guest Relations.

Admission Fees – One-day/one-park ticket: $42–$52. Children under 3 years of age get in free. Parking: $7 *(free for guests staying at Disney properties)*.

Park Hopper tickets *(for 5 days)* are also available, as is an Annual Passport *(unlimited admission to all 4 parks)*. Check *www.disneyworld.com* for most current fees. Same-day re-entry is permitted with a valid ticket and a hand stamp.

> **Your Visit**
> On the day of your visit, arrive at the park when ticket booths open, usually one hour before the scheduled opening time. With your ticket, you will receive a Walt Disney World Resort guide, detailed map and show schedule that lists times for performances, parades and all other entertainment. All guided tours are limited to 15–20 people; prices are in addition to park entrance fees; advance reservations are required *(939-8687)*.

The free, computerized **FASTPASS®** system allows you to skip lines at 24 attractions. Simply insert your theme-park ticket into the turn-style and you'll get a FASTPASS with a time to return. When you return, go directly to the attraction through the FASTPASS entrance.

Park Hours – Each park has individual hours. In general, Disney's Animal Kingdom opens at 8am; the other three Disney parks open at 9am *(Epcot's World Showcase opens at 11am; 10am in summer)*. Disney water parks open at 10am. Closing hours vary seasonally and depend upon the day's events. Call the park or check www.disneyworld.com before your trip to obtain the current hours for the month in which you intend to visit.

When To Go – Walt Disney World is busiest during the summer, Christmas and spring holidays. The least crowded period falls between Thanksgiving and December 25, followed by September and October, then January. Monday, Tuesday and Wednesday—except during holiday seasons—are the busiest days of the week at Magic Kingdom. Tuesday and Wednesday are more crowded at Epcot; attendance at Disney-MGM Studios is heaviest on Thursday and Friday. Sunday morning tends to be least crowded at all the parks.

Getting There From the Airport – Shuttle service to Walt Disney World Resort from Orlando International Airport departs from the baggage-claim area year-round daily *(every 15–20min; $16 one-way)*. If you're driving from Orlando airport, take the Beeline Expressway *(Rte. 528 West; toll)*, then continue on I-4 West to the parks.

Must Know: Practical Information

Getting There By Car – Walt Disney World Resort is located 20mi southwest of downtown Orlando. Take I-4 West to Exit 67B for the best access to Epcot, Typhoon Lagoon, Downtown Disney and River Country. For the most direct route to Disney's Animal Kingdom, Disney's Wide World of Sports, Disney-MGM Studios and the Magic Kingdom, take Exit 64B (Rte. 192 West) and follow signs to the various parks. Trams shuttle visitors to the main gates from pick-up areas throughout the sprawling parking lots. *Be sure to note the section and row where you park; it's easy to lose track of your vehicle.*

Staying Inside The Disney Complex – The vast Walt Disney World Resort complex offers approximately 30,000 rooms at nearly 30 properties that in-clude resort hotels, villas, condominiums, cabins and campgrounds. Rates vary depending on location, type of hotel and season; rates are lower during early Jan–mid-Feb, mid-Apr–mid-Jun and Sept–mid-Dec. Children under 18 stay free in rooms with parents. In-room baby-sitting service is available. KinderCare center accepts 1- to 4-year-old children. For all reservations, call 934-7639; dial *88 from specially marked phones; or visit the Guest Relations booths at individual parks.

Getting Around – Monorail trains, buses, ferry boats and water taxis *(all free)* link all attractions including hotels and resorts throughout the Disney complex. Buses operate approximately every 20min, starting 1hr prior to park opening until closing. Routes painted in red are direct routes after 4pm. The only excep-tions: Service to Magic Kingdom, Epcot, Disney-MGM Studios from Disney's Old Key West Resort and the Disney Institute operate on scheduled pick-up times between noon and 6pm. Service to Blizzard Beach Water Park operates on a schedule with up to a 35-minute interval between buses on some routes.

Dining – Inside the complex, you can choose among a wide selection of eat-eries. Sidewalk stalls sell fresh fruit, hot dogs, ice cream and snacks; cafeterias and carryout stands accommodate diners on the run; more expensive restau-rants mirror the theme of the parks in which they are located (make reserva-tions early in the day by contacting Guest Relations). Dining at any of the Disney Resort hotels and dinner shows is open to the public; for priority seating, be sure to make reservations *(939-3463)*.

Disney By Night

During the summer months and on holidays, visitors are treated to nightly extravaganzas of lights, lasers and fireworks at the three original parks:

- **SpectroMagic**, a stellar parade of lighted floats, makes its way down Main Street, U.S.A. twice each evening.
- **Fantasy in the Sky** fireworks transform the Magic Kingdom into a wonderland to the tune of "When You Wish Upon a Star."
- **IllumiNations**, held around the lagoon at Epcot, showcases a breathtaking display of lasers, fountains, music and fireworks.
- **Fantasmic!** is a boisterous and popular laser-and-water display at Disney-MGM Studios.

Consult park entertainment schedules for locations and show times.

Sports & Entertainment – Enjoy a round of **golf** on one of Disney's six championship courses *($60–$170; for tee times, call 824-2270)*. Other recreational opportunities available to the general public and Disney Resort guests include tennis, boating, fishing, a health club, swimming, waterskiing and horseback riding. Youth Education Series programs focus on nature, art, culture and ecology *(939-2223)*.

A variety of live-performance **stage shows** are presented in the parks throughout the day. All operate on a first-come, first-served basis. For times, check the show schedule at each park. **Disney Character Breakfasts** take place daily at various resort hotels and at all four parks; make reservations up to 60 days in advance *(939-3463; see Musts for Kids)*.

For **shopping**, head to **Downtown Disney Marketplace** *(entrance to the Marketplace is at the intersection of Hotel Plaza Blvd. & Buena Vista Dr.; 407-824-4321; www.downtowndisney.com)*, where myriad shops sell everything Disney.

Important Phone Numbers	
Emergency (24hrs)	**911**
Police (non-emergency)	246-4141
Medical Services, House Calls USA	800-468-3537
24hr Dentist	903-0320
24-hour Pharmacies	
Walgreens, 2420 E. Colonial Dr.	894-6781
CVS, 3502 Edgewater Dr.	245-1001
Poison Control	800-222-1222
Time/Weather	676-3131
Walt Disney World Resort Information	824-4321
Disney Hotel and Dinner Show Reservations	934-7639
Disney Resort Dining and Recreation	939-3463
Lost & Found (same day)	
Magic Kingdom	824-4521
Epcot	560-6105
Disney-MGM Studios	560-3764
Disney's Animal Kingdom	938-2265
Central Lost and Found	824-4245

Orlando

A Cinderella Story: Orlando, Florida

Set smack-dab in the center of the Sunshine State, Orlando is one of the most popular tourist destinations in the US. A visit to Walt Disney World, the theme park that put Orlando on the map, is practically a requirement for families with children. Surprisingly, the park is also a honeymoon hotspot—a major bridal magazine named the city the number-one choice in the world for starry-eyed couples. Where Disney went, other parks soon followed, and now the Orlando area is home to Universal Studios and Universal's Islands of Escape, SeaWorld, and more, attracting some 43 million visitors annually.

The city of Orlando itself, the state's largest inland city, serves as the commercial hub of Central Florida. Superhighways lined with chain hotels, resort complexes, eateries and discount shopping malls now web the flat, lake-dotted subtropical landscape, but historic neighborhoods still grace the older portions of cities and towns in the region.

Just outside Orlando the pace slows, and the landscape becomes more rural. The nearby towns of Lakeland and Lake Wales, for example, sit at the heart of the state's citrus-growing region and offer a quieter ambience—and a sense of what Central Florida was like decades ago.

Before there were tourists wearing caps with mouse ears, there were settlers wearing cowboy hats—mostly north Florida cattlemen who were attracted to the area's lush grasslands. To protect pioneers during the Second Seminole War, the US government established several forts in the area. The settlement that arose around Fort Gatlin (1838) formed the nucleus of the future city of Orlando. By the 1860s the emerging town occupied part of a vast cotton plantation. The citrus industry sprouted in the 1880s when the new South Florida Railway gave local growers access to wider markets. Orlando remained largely an orange-blossom-scented agricultural town through the first half of the 20C. Then a fellow named Disney came to town and forever changed the face of the city *(see sidebar)*.

Today the Orlando boom shows no signs of slowing. Demographic and financial forecasters predict that, together with Walt Disney World's continual expansion, Universal Orlando's plans to triple the size of its complex, and the city's appeal

The Dawning of Disney

In 1965, having secretly purchased almost 300,000 acres in Orange and Osceola counties, **Walt Disney** (1901–1966), animated-film wizard and creator of California's Disneyland, announced plans to build a theme park outside Orlando. Overnight, land values in the area skyrocketed. Throughout the rest of the decade, development engulfed the communities to the southwest along the I-4 corridor. Walt Disney World opened to great fanfare in 1971. SeaWorld followed two years later, and Universal Studios Florida joined the local theme-park ranks in 1990. In the years between, metropolitan Orlando tripled its population. It now boasts the largest concentration of hotel rooms in the US and ranks as one of the top commercial tourist destinations in the world.

With the theme parks came endless outlet malls, restaurants and entertainment facilities and, with them, more jobs: service-sector employment has increased nearly 138 percent within the past decade. A number of major corporations have made Orlando their headquarters as well. Even Hollywood has moved east, sort of, with Universal, MGM-Disney, and Nickelodeon Studios filming dozens of movies and television shows in O-Town.

as a convention center, Orlando will continue to be one of the country's fastest-growing areas well into the 21C. Orlando ranks among the top five US cities in terms of the number of conventions hosted each year. In addition, one of Orlando's major thoroughfares, International Drive, has increasingly become an attraction unto itself, lined as it is with dozens of restaurants and smaller tourist haunts.

Happily, there are still a few signs of "Old Orlando" left, if you know where to look. Delightfully cheesy roadside attractions like Gatorland still exist, where the highlight of a visit is watching handlers hand-feed chicken parts to snappish gators. You can still get a look at Central Florida's swamplands and paddle a real river, the Wekiva, about a half-hour out of town. You may even see a few birds and critters as you cruise. True, they won't appear on command or crack jokes like their theme-park counterparts, but these hardy creatures were on the scene long before Disney's Animal Kingdom arrived!

Theme Parks

Isn't this why you came to Orlando in the first place—to wait in line in the sweltering heat, to scare yourself silly on crazy coasters and other thrill rides, and to listen to the kids whine 'cuz they didn't get to meet Mickey? Oh, come on, now, it's not that bad. Relax and get in touch with your inner child! From Cinderella to Shamu, there never needs to be a dull moment in Orlando.

Magic Kingdom★★★

Take I-4 West to Exit 64B (US-192 West). Turn right on World Dr. and follow signs to park entrance. 407-824-4321. www.disneyworld.com. In general, the park is open year-round daily 9am; closing times vary. $52 ages 10 & over, $42 ages 3–9.

At the Magic Kingdom, it's all about magic: the Gothic splendor of Cinderella Castle, the look on a child's face when he or she first meets Mickey, the stomach-plunging pleasure of Space Mountain as it hurtles through darkness. And only a true curmudgeon could resist the legions of multicolored animated children trilling "It's a Small World After All." For most guests, the Magic Kingdom is the sweet little heart of Walt Disney World, so adorable, you'll forgive it the crowds, the heat, and the Main Street Bakery that always runs out of Nestle Tollhouse Cookies.

Not such a small world after all, the 107-acre park includes seven areas that radiate out from the Central Plaza in front of Cinderella Castle. Shops (all selling roughly the same merchandise), eateries, attractions, and costumed "cast members" (ride attendants, shop keepers) in each area echo the dominant theme of their "land." The main goings-on here are meet-and-greets with favorite Disney characters, cutesy, retro rides that are sprinkled around the park (like Pirates of the Caribbean), and thrill rides. The latter are easy to identify: they have 'mountain' in their name (Space Mountain, Splash Mountain, Big Thunder Mountain). Coasters have gotten a lot hairier since these rides were built, but the Magic Kingdom mainstays are still major crowd-pleasers—the long lines say it all. Then there's the ultra-icky ExtraTERRORestrial Alien Encounter and the corny "Bear-itones" of Country Bear Jamboree. If you've made it this far, reward yourself with the Magic Kingdom's signature treat, a turkey leg the size of your head (just don't count on a tollhouse cookie for dessert).

MAIN STREET, U.S.A.

Tiny Victorian storefronts (housing modern-day Mickey Mouse-logoed goods) re-create the milieu of an early 19C town. Adding to the Americana atmosphere, a horse-drawn trolley, antique fire engine, omnibus, "horseless carriages" and jitneys carry passengers between the Town Square and Central Plaza. Minstrels often stroll the street, and the Share a Dream Come True Parade wends its way down Main Street every afternoon, highlighting characters and themes from Disney animated films. During evenings in peak periods *(summer & Christmas holidays)*, the SpectroMagic parade fills the street with a dazzling spectacle of Disney characters and special

---

Honey, I Shrunk the Building

In designing Main Street, U.S.A., Walt Disney used a film device called forced perspective: Upper stories of buildings are not as high as lower ones, giving the buildings a taller appearance.

---

effects. The parade is often followed by Fantasy in the Sky, featuring a flying Tinkerbell and a fireworks display.

Too pooped to pop? Board the Walt Disney World Railroad, one of the steam trains that circle the park, with stops at Frontierland (home of Splash Mountain and Big Thunder Mountain) and Mickey's Toontown Fair (Disney character central). *Check park brochure for parade show times.*

ADVENTURELAND

A psychedelic fusion of Polynesian, Moorish, French Colonial and Spanish Colonial architecture marks this peculiar little land. Skip the Tiki Birds and the Swiss Family Tree House (the former is just plain weird; the latter is a nightmare of lost children) and, instead, ride **Pirates of the Caribbean** over and over again.

Big Thunder Mountain Railroad

This classic, clackety coaster is themed as a runaway train in an old mining town. It gathers steam as it spirals around a mountain, negotiates a series of hoodoos, caves and canyons, then plunges down a dark, rickety mine shaft. Back in its day, this was considered a pretty wild ride; now it seems fairly tame. To ratchet up the thrill level, ride Big Thunder Mountain at night.

Jungle Cruise

If only for nostalgia's sake, float down this jungle river that loosely resembles the landscapes of Africa, Asia and South America. Pop-up critters include hippos, elephants and crocodiles, while the captain keeps things moving with pun-laced narration.

Magic Carpets of Aladdin

Board a magic carpet for a ride around a mammoth Genie lamp, while trying to avoid water-squirting camels.

Pirates of the Caribbean

Disney does naughty, with this Caribbean village peopled by delightfully debauched pirates. Boat-riding passengers cruise past a series of sets where lifelike buccaneers chase women, drink rum, and enjoy a bit of the hardy har-har, alongside pigs and parrots. This is one of the most popular amusement rides ever created, and it's easy to see why. Disney designers used their own faces as models for the pirates' mugs.

Splash Mountain

Riders board dugouts for a languid float through the swamps and bayous of Splash Mountain, as Br'er Rabbit, Br'er Fox and other characters from the 1946 Disney classic *Song of the South* serenade passing vessels. At the mountaintop, there's a delicious pause, then a thrilling drop down a 52ft, 47-degree flume that delivers a soaking at the bottom.

FANTASYLAND

With the fairy-tale air of an old European village, the original Fantasyland in California was Walt Disney's personal favorite. While the Orlando version lacks some of the quaintness of the original, it still ranks as the most beloved area in all of Walt Disney World. Adults with a taste for whimsy are captivated by its old-fashioned magic, as are young children who have seen the Disney classics. (Most of the rides in Fantasyland are based on Disney films like *Snow White* and *Peter Pan*.) Live shows take place frequently at the **Castle Forecourt Stage** and at **Fantasyland Pavilion**.

Did You Know?

Cinderella Castle was inspired by Neuschwanstein, one of the 19C castles built in the Bavaria region of Germany by King Ludwig II.

Cinderella Castle

Ornamented with turrets, towers, gold spires and leaded-glass windows, this 189ft-high Gothic extravaganza reigns supreme among Disney castles worldwide. Sad to say, you can't go inside the castle unless you spring for a meal at the restaurant, but you can admire the detailed mosaics inside the arched entrance of the castle gate. These depict the rags-to-riches story of Cinderella.

Hall of Presidents

The show begins with an unabashedly patriotic film on the history of the US Constitution. Next, the Presidents appear (or audio-animatronic versions of them), for roll call and snippets of famous speeches.

Haunted Mansion

Ghosts and ghoulies populate the creepy mansion that looms ominously along the shore of the Rivers of America. From the "stretchroom," where heights and dimensions are not what they seem, visitors board "doom buggies" for a semi-scary trip among holographic images and haunting-but-humorous special effects.

It's a Small World

This cross-cultural fantasy was conceived for the 1964 World's Fair and embodies an idealized view of international harmony. Aboard small boats, passengers float past 500 audio-animatronic children and animals representing nearly 100 nations—each child singing a theme song that's guaranteed to stay in your head for days.

Liberty Square

Patriotic Liberty Square re-creates a brick and clapboard colonial town, set around a central square. Cast from the same mold as the revered original, a Liberty Bell sits in the center of the square. A 130-plus-year-old live oak, discovered on the Disney property, was transplanted here, and designated as the site's "liberty tree."

Mad Tea Party

Sure it's a tilt-a-whirl, but it's the cutest one ever created. Passengers board giant teacups, and control the amount of spin themselves, from tame to stomach-wrenchingly dizzying.

Peter Pan's Flight

Winning points for artistic concept is this sweet little ride, where riders board pirate-ship gondolas and float

> ### SRO for Country Bears
>
> Planning to catch the wildly popular Country Bear Jamboree? Arrive early—these cornball songfests fill up fast.

out of the Darling children's bedroom above a fiber-optic version of nighttime London. Soon after, passengers plunge into Never Never Land, where Captain Hook, Smee and the Lost Boys await in their galleon.

Snow White's Adventures

Beware the Wicked Queen as you ride through the Seven Dwarfs' cozy cottage to an encounter with a poisoned-apple-wielding villainess, and on to a happy ending.

FRONTIERLAND

The Old West lives on in this faux frontier town. If you hear gunfire, no need to duck—just look toward the rooftops where gunslingers frequently stage rambunctious mock shoot-outs. Most guests head here to ride Splash Mountain (a flume ride) or Big Thunder Mountain. This is also the place to sit for a spell, by catching a dancehall show at

the **Diamond Horseshoe Saloon Revue**, or to see those wholesome hairy pranksters, the country bears of **Country Bear Jamboree**.

Theme Parks

TOMORROWLAND

Even Disney's Imagineers (design/techno whizzes) couldn't predict the future, so they gave up on the futuristic theme when they overhauled Tomorrowland a few years ago. Instead, they fashioned a "fantasy future city," capturing the futuristic visions of the 1920s and 30s. Design-wise, it has a cool, Jetson-y appeal, and it's worth a wander, if only to ride Space Mountain.

Astro Orbiter

Pilot your own orbiter through swirling planets around Tomorrowland's colorful central spire. Although popular with the younger set, the updated ride affords adults good views of the Magic Kingdom.

Buzz Lightyear's Space Ranger Spin

This interactive space fantasy teams visitors with characters from *Toy Story* in defending Earth's battery supply against the evil Emperor Zurg. Piloting your own XP-38 Space Cruiser equipped with twin laser cannons, you zap and steer your way to "infinity and beyond." As combatants fire the infrared lasers, targets spring to animated life.

ExtraTERRORestrial Alien Encounter

Word has it, this little gross-o-rama wasn't scary enough when it was first conceived, so Michael Eisner sent the designers back to the drawing board. The result: an 18-minute sci-fi scenario designed with a little help from special effects guru George Lucas. Inside the Interplanetary Convention Center you'll meet a maniacal corporation executive from another planet who attempts to demonstrate his new technique of intergalactic teleportation. Then, of course, "something goes terribly wrong," (a recurring theme on these rides) and a hideous alien space creature mistakenly materializes. The ensuing blitz of sound, light and other special-effects-in-the-dark are scary, and so yucky, you'll think a team of 12-year-old boys was behind all this.

Space Mountain

Since it opened in 1975, this roller coaster—enclosed in a futuristic mountain—is one of Disney's most popular rides. Not for the faint of heart, Space Mountain hurtles passengers through near-darkness, plunging them into sudden, atmospheric comet showers and past faintly twinkling stars.

Timekeeper

Guided by a madcap robot (with voice supplied by Robin Williams), spectators travel through time via a 360-degree movie, passing from the age of dinosaurs into the future. Along the way you'll meet such historical figures as Mozart, Leonardo da Vinci, and H.G. Wells, as the camera swoops through breathtaking scenery from around the world.

TOONTOWN

Scaled to the younger set (kids under 10—and their parents), this whimsical village with its pastel-colored, round-edged buildings has a sort of gingerbread appeal.

Mickey's Toontown Fair

Toontown occupies a relatively quiet, three-acre corner of the Kingdom. Scaled to visitors under age 10 (accompanied by their parents, of course), the whimsical village is all gingerbread curlicues and pastel hues. For kids who want to meet their favorite Disney characters, this is the place.

Mickey's Country House

A stroll through Mickey's cozy home gives kids a peek at the lifestyle of Disney's Big Cheese, even a look at his grocery list. A corridor leads to a sound-stage and theater, where Mickey himself (now in his 70s but blessed with a Dick Clark-like agelessness) holds court backstage, signing autographs for fans. *Mickey is unavailable during parade times.*

Minnie's Country House

Opposite Mickey's house is Minnie's quaint pink bachelorette pad, where Mickey's better half seems stuck in the 1950s with a houseful of appliances. Across the lane is Donald Duck's boat, the *Miss Daisy* (sort of a nautical Jungle Jim) and a kiddie coaster, **The Barnstormer at Goofy's Wiseacre Farm.**

Disney Without The Wait

Horrendous lines have long been a fact of life at Disney parks. Happily, they're trying to do something about it. They've installed something called **FASTPASS®** at their most popular rides and shows.

Here's how it works: Early in the day, you go to the Fastpass turnstile, located in front of the ride or show, insert your park ticket into a slot, and out comes a FASTPASS ticket, telling you when to return. At the appointed time, return to the attraction and head for the FASTPASS entrance, sprinting past the hordes of folks standing in the regular line. True, it's not too spontaneous, but it does provide some structure to your day.

Not surprisingly, Universal has come up with a similar system called **Universal Express**. Now if they could just do something about the lines at the front entrance . . .

Toontown Hall of Fame

Combine the charm of a country-fair tent with the commercial aspects of a Disney store, and this is what you get. At the "character greeting location," indefatigable Goofy, Pluto and the gang shake hands with the kiddies, pose for pictures, and scrawl autographs with their big mitts.

Epcot★★★

Take I-4 West to Exit 67B; go west on Epcot Center Dr. and follow signs to park entrance on left. 407-824-4321. www.disneyworld.com. In general Epcot is open year-round daily 9am; closing times vary. World Showcase is open daily 11am (10am during summer months). $52 ages 10 & over, $42 ages 3–9.

Walt Disney envisioned this property as an "experimental prototype community of to-morrow" (aka EPCOT) and a showcase of American creativity. Unveiled in 1982, the 260-acre park is divided into two areas: Future World, housing pavilions devoted to technology and ingenuity, and World Showcase, celebrating the culture and architecture of 11 nations. After years of being rather ho-hum, Future World is hot again with the addition of **Test Track**, a cool, General Motors-sponsored thrill ride, and **Mission: SPACE**, a simulated astronaut adventure. World Showcase remains *the* place to eat on Planet Disney.

FUTURE WORLD

Eight large pavilions encircle the 180ft-high faceted geosphere that has come to symbolize Epcot. Sponsored by major American corporations, pavilions house rides, interactive displays and films, all saluting humankind's technological achievements.

Honey, I Shrunk the Audience

This totally goofy 3-D movie is worth 20 minutes of your time—plus, you get to sit down. It's nice escapism for kids, too, especially if you've made them endure the sex-education film, *The Making of Me*.

Mission: SPACE

Future World's newest attraction is a simulated astronaut adventure, where guests can experience weightlessness and other effects of outer space.

Spaceship Earth

Spiral up 18 stories in a time-machine vehicle inside Epcot's giant globe, where you'll ride past animated scenes depicting the history of human communication. (It's more interesting than it sounds—and you want to get inside that sphere, right?)

Test Track

Buckle up; it's going to be a bumpy ride, as you "road test" an experimental car for speed, road handling, impact testing (the most fun) and suspension. OK for non-drivers and bad drivers—you don't *really* drive.

WORLD SHOWCASE

The 1.3mi promenade at World Showcase circles a 40-acre lagoon and features pavilions representing 11 different cultures. Each pavilion—staffed by folks who actually hale from each of these nations—offers a sampling of foods, architecture, crafts and traditions of the culture it represents. Expect plenty of live music, a lot of food (some of it really good, if pricey) and a couple of movies and rides in this leisurely, and adult-oriented theme park.

American Adventure

Set in the middle of World Showcase, a five-story brick building serves as the host pavilion. Architecture owes a debt to Independence Hall, Boston's Old State House, and Monticello. A multimedia show, **The American Adventure**, features lifelike audio-animatronics versions of Ben Franklin and Mark Twain.

Canada

Celebrating Canada's cultural diversity, this pavilion features a model of a 19C French chateau, totem poles and a longhouse, even a log-hewn trading post. Don't miss the film **O Canada!** It's a 360-degree whirlwind of gorgeous North Country scenery.

China

You won't overlook this one. The shimmering opulence of Beijing's Temple of Heaven (replicated in half size) overlooks a Chinese garden, where koi shimmer through a pond crossed by elegant walkways. Inside, catch the 360-degree film **Wonders of China: Land of Beauty, Land of Time** for dazzling visuals.

France

This land evokes turn-of-the-century Paris, with its mansard-roofed buildings, and a mini (one-tenth its actual size) Eiffel Tower. The outdoor cafe is always abustle, but real foodies head upstairs, to **Bistro de Paris**, for gourmet French cuisine created by noted chefs Paul Bocuse, Roger Vergé, and Gaston Lenôtre.

Big-Name Chefs, Tiny Tab

Hankering for fabulous French cooking, inspired by top toques Bocuse, Vergé and Lenôtre? Skip Bistro de Paris (which features an upscale menu with entrées priced at $28 and up) and go to **Les Chefs de France.** Located downstairs in the same building, **Les Chefs** reflects the influences of these same superstar chefs, but at down-to-earth prices (entrées range from $13.95 to about $25.95).

Germany

A facade modeled after the castles in Eltz and Stahleck is the backdrop for cobblestone St. Georgesplatz, a square named for its prominent statue of St. George and the Dragon. Turreted structures of a German village surround the plaza, where a traditional glockenspiel chimes each hour. Then there's the oom-pah band and a biergarten, which always hops on a sultry afternoon.

Italy

In this plaza, Venice's Piazza San Marco is re-created with reproductions of the Doge's Palace and an angel-topped brick campanile. Antiqued facades, an open-air market and a Bernini-inspired fountain add to the dolce vita atmosphere. The main activity here is—surprise!—eating, especially at **L'Originale Alfredo Di Roma Ristorante**, based on the Rome restaurant where fettuccine Alfredo originated.

Japan

Landscaped with peaceful water and rock gardens and evergreens, this pavilion captures the contemplative serenity of traditional Japan. The most prominent feature is a vivid blue five-story pagoda based on the 8C Horyuji Temple in Nara. Shoppers head to the **Mitsukoshi Department Store**, dating back to the 17C and housed in a reproduction of Kyoto's Gosho Imperial Palace. Indulge in a sake martini on the second floor of the store, at **Matsunoma Lounge**.

Mexico

Hands-down the most romantic ride at Disney World, **El Rio del Tiempo** takes passengers on a meandering boat ride down the River of Time through a history of Mexico, from smoking volcanoes to the modern landscapes of Mexico City.

The Ride's Great, The Food's Better

Doing El Rio del Tiempo at World Showcase Mexico? Then do lunch at the enchanting **San Angel Inn Restaurant**. Specialties include *huachinango a la Veracruzana* (red snapper poached in wine with tomatoes, onions and chilies) and *mole poblano* (chicken in a spicy sauce made with Mexican chocolate).

Morocco

Elaborate tilework and carvings crafted by Moroccan artists help to create a dazzling re-creation of the sights, smells and sounds of this North African country. Fronted by a replica of Marrakech's famous Koutoubia Minaret, the pavilion is divided into a new and old medina, or city. The narrow, exotic casbah opens into a formal Moroccan eatery, **Restaurant Marrakesh,** offering good food (but largely ignored by the Epcot throngs).

Norway

So what if they sell Norwegian wool sweaters in sweltering Orlando? Norway offers a replica of a 12C house of worship, a small cobblestone plaza, and **Maelstrom**, a boat ride through Norway with a few surprises thrown in.

United Kingdom

Beatles impersonators crooning Fab Four hits, a replica of Anne Hathaway's thatched-roof cottage—this must be Great Britain! The clubby **Rose & Crown Pub** lures passersby with pub standards like cottage pie and room-temp lagers.

Disney's Animal Kingdom★★★

Take I-4 West to Exit 64B. Go west on US-192, right (north) on World Dr. and left (west) on Osceola Pkwy., then follow signs to parking plaza. 407-824-4321. www.disneyworld.com. In general, open year-round daily 8am; closing times vary. $52 ages 10 & over, $42 ages 3–9.

Disney's newest theme park is devoted to the natural world: animals living and extinct, as well as "creatures of the imagination" (their words). Geographically the largest park, Animal Kingdom boasts 1,000 animals of 200 species and four million plants on more than 500 acres of land. Whimsy meets reality here, as visitors move from animated insects (**It's Tough to Be a Bug**) to real-life critters undergoing surgical procedures (**Rafiki's Planet Watch**). Of course, there are the usual shows and places to meet-and-greet Disney characters, but the real stars here are the animals you'll glimpse on **Kilimanjaro Safaris**, the main event at this park, and the carved images in the enormous **Tree of Life**, the park's centerpiece.

You can easily do this park in a day. Or, if you're not all that animal-crazed, skip the theme park altogether and spring for a room at the **Animal Kingdom Lodge**, where—big secret revealed here—the critters head back in late afternoon after their day at the park, and guests can spot them from the lodge.

AFRICA

Shop owners peddle their wares from marketplace stalls in this fairly authentic representation of a coastal Kenyan community. White-coral walls and reed-thatched roofs typify the Arab-influenced architecture.

Tips For Visiting

Once you step off that safari jeep, it's tough to find your way around this megapark. Here's a cheat sheet: Animal Kingdom extends in four directions from its hub, the Tree of Life, in the heart of Discovery Island. The two most popular attractions, Kilimanjaro Safaris and Dinosaur, are at opposite ends of the park (make a beeline to one of these upon arrival to beat the crowds). Two live shows, currently, Festival of the Lion King and Tarzan Rocks! are presented in large, open-air amphitheaters. Expect long lines for the 3-D film *It's Tough to Be a Bug* beneath the Tree of Life. As you head toward Discovery Island from Animal Kingdom's main gateway, you'll first pass through the Oasis, a lush botanical garden whose grottoes are inhabited by brightly colored macaws, miniature deer, iguanas, tree kangaroos and other unusual creatures. Access Discovery Island via footbridges from other areas of the park.

Theme Parks

Kilimanjaro Safaris

These backcountry safaris are the reason most folks spring for a ticket to the Animal Kingdom. Oversized all-terrain trucks carry passengers down a rutted, twisting dirt road, across river fords and through tropical forests, to the grasslands of the Serengeti Plain. Assisted by a bush pilot/game warden (who flies ahead as a wildlife spotter), travelers look for rhinoceroses, elephants, lions, cheetahs, zebras, giraffes, baboons, gazelles, antelopes and other residents of the savanna. Of course, "something goes terribly wrong" (this is, after all, a Disney ride)—a bridge almost collapses, poachers are spotted—but all turns out well in the end (this is, after all, a Disney ride).

Pangani Forest Exploration Trail

A self-guided trail through a bamboo jungle offers close-up views (through acrylic windows) of lowland gorillas, hippopotami (underwater) and exotic birds.

Rafiki's Planet Watch

Board the Wildlife Express—a 19C narrow-gauge steam train—to an animal-care facility and a children's petting zoo (they call it the "affection section"). Here you'll find animal demonstrations and high-tech exhibits highlighting rain forest destruction and conservation efforts around the world. If you can handle it, look through a window into an operating room where veterinarians perform surgical procedures on park animals.

ASIA

At this re-created rural village nestled in the rain forest, guests take on the **Maharajah Jungle Trek**, a walking tour that winds past decaying temple ruins. Look for glimpses of Bengal tigers, Komodo dragons and other creatures roaming in the lush vegetation. Beyond that, Asia is home to the popular **Kali River Rapids**, a whitewater thrill ride.

Flights of Wonder

The avian talents of falcons, macaws, ibis and other birds are featured in this free-flying show at the Caravan Stage. The story line features a treasure-seeking youth and a mythical phoenix. This is a good place to settle in when you're weary of trekking, and there's seldom a wait.

Kali River Rapids

Every Disney park has its requisite water ride—and it's a good thing, too. This is Orlando, where sweltering temperatures and egg-frying-hot asphalt rule the day. This wet-and-wild ride takes you through the foaming rapids of the Clakrandi River. Along the way you'll be bumped, dipped and properly drenched.

CAMP MINNIE-MICKEY

Designed to resemble an Adirondack summer camp, this is the perfect place for small fry to interact with their favorite Disney characters. "Green rooms"—jungle and forest canopies—serve as greeting areas where Mickey, Winnie the Pooh, and characters from *The Lion King* and *Jungle Book* sign autographs.

Festival of the Lion King

This splashy show features 50 performers in African tribal garb or animal costumes, singing, dancing and performing aerial acrobatics on four giant stages. The finale of the show is an audience sing-along of "The Lion Sleeps Tonight," led by Simba himself.

Grandma Willow's Grove

The musical presented here is called "Pocahontas and Her Forest Friends," which pretty much says it all. Beloved by four-year-olds, tolerated by indulgent parents, the show's message is, the only animal that can save the forests and their inhabitants is—you guessed it!—humans.

DINOLAND U.S.A.

This faux research camp/paleontology dig offers a livelier, more child-friendly tone than the rest of Animal Kingdom, with a playground called **The Boneyard**, a rowdy rock-and-roll show, and a couple of fun rides.

Dinosaur

Visitors who board the 12-passenger "Time Rover" are sent by a deranged scientist back to late-Cretaceous times to bring home a living dinosaur, just before an asteroid is due to strike the planet and wipe out all life. Got all that? Doesn't matter—you'll have a fine time dodging dinos and narrowly escaping meteoric catastrophe on this high-tech motion-simulator ride.

What's For Lunch?

Animal Kingdom has an outpost of the **Rainforest Café,** but after hanging around a theme park, do you really need gigantic flapping butterflies, faux thunderstorms and automated gorillas? For a break from the overload, head to the humble **Flame Tree Barbecue,** where they smoke their own meats, make their own sauce and serve it up at (relatively) modest prices.

Primeval Whirl

Board this cute, curvy coaster at Chester and Hester's Dino-Rama and spin yourself silly. It's a hybrid coaster and tilt-a-whirl, and it's a gas.

Tarzan Rocks!

Perfect for pre-teens, this live stage show features an impossibly buff Tarzan and an impossibly skinny Jane, upstaged by a swarm of flip-happy in-line skaters. Rock music and aerial stunts make this a fast-paced 30 minutes (although what all this has to do with dinosaurs is anyone's guess).

DISCOVERY ISLAND

Fashioned as a tropical artists' colony, Discovery Island is home to roving musicians, puppeteers and storytellers, and a multicultural coterie of crafters and artisans.

Tree of Life

This giant (145ft-tall) man-made tree features 325 intricately carved images of mammals, birds, reptiles, amphibians and insects. Adapted from Disney's animated feature *The Lion King*, the tree celebrates all creatures (remember the theme song, "The Circle of Life"?). The tree is visible from points throughout the park. At its base, birds and small animals gather.

It's Tough to Be a Bug

A delightful cast of animated insects and arachnids express the harsh "reality" of their lives in a theater set beneath the roots of the Tree of Life. Meanwhile, the audience, wearing 3-D glasses, experiences such special effects as termite sneezes (you'll get wet), stinkbug emissions (euww!) and a cloud of pesticide (fog).

Disney MGM Studios ★★★

Take I-4 West to Exit 67B. Go west on Epcot Center Dr. and turn left on Buena Vista Dr. Follow sings to park entrance on left. Alternate access via Exit 64B (US-192 West); turn right on World Dr. and follow signs to entrance on right. 407-824-4321. www.disneyworld.com. In general open year-round daily 9am; closing times vary. $52 ages 10 & over, $42 ages 3–9.

Totally charming, not too crowded, and easy to get around—these are among the virtues of Disney MGM Studios. This theme-park-cum-movie-studio celebrates the art of filmmaking, from animation and stuntcraft to adventure and romance. Done up in cool Art Deco design, the 154-acre site re-creates the look of Hollywood in its 1930s and 40s heyday. Sophisticated techniques meet playful style here, where audience members are often called upon to make cameo appearances in live shows. This one you can do in a leisurely day, especially if you skip the warmed-over TV show attractions and ho-hum shows (i.e., Disney's The Hunchback of Notre Dame: A Musical Adventure) and focus instead on the real classics. These include **The Great Movie Ride**, **Twilight Zone Tower of Terror** and, of course, **Star Tours**.

Just walking around this place will put a smile on your face, though. It's all palm trees and sleek style on **Hollywood Boulevard**, home to a pagoda-roofed replica of Mann's Chinese Theater in Los Angeles. You'll even see the famous footprints-in-cement. Meanwhile, over on **Sunset Boulevard**, the street is lined with Mediterranean Revival facades, antique autos and fruit vendors in Depression-era garb, while Glenn Miller music plays in the background. At the neon-lit movie palace, Mickey and friends sign autographs and pose for pictures. (Also look for Mickey in the soundstages of Mickey Avenue, and the courtyard around the Sorcerer Hat icon.)

After dark, everybody heads to Sunset Boulevard for the **Fantasmic!** laser light show. If you don't arrive early enough to get in, you can console yourself at **Aerosmith's Rock 'n' Roller Coaster** (awesome at night, and the lines are shorter).

Dining in the Movies

Even the restaurants carry the theme, and they're a hoot. The **50's Prime Time Café** looks like Beaver Cleaver's kitchen. The TV is tuned to 1950s sitcoms, and Mom won't give you dessert unless you've cleaned your plate. Over at the **Sci-Fi Dine-In Theater Restaurant,** you sit in a vintage 50s convertible and watch cheesy sci-fi movie clips while you dine, under a canopy of fiber-optic stars. In either case, the food isn't nearly as memorable as the setting, but go for the experience.

Aerosmith's Rock 'n' Roller Coaster

You won't see Steven Tyler on this ride, but boy, you'll hear him! You climb inside a lightning-fast limo and hurtle from zero to 60mph in less than three seconds, with a few wild turns and upside-down twists thrown in for good measure. The effect is amplified by the Aerosmith tunes pounding out of the speakers. What this has to do with the movies, who knows, unless Tyler has a Disney movie deal under wraps.

Beauty and the Beast—Live on Stage

Unexpectedly romantic fare, this take-off on the Disney animated film of the same name features lip-synching cups and pots and a great girl-meets-Beast story line, with lively song and dance routines.

Fantasmic!

Sorcerer Mickey takes on wicked villains in this action-packed nighttime show. A classic show-down between good and evil, the eye-popping extravaganza features lasers, pyrotechnics and dancing waters, all set to rousing Disney music. Don't bring small children if you can avoid it— this show is really loud.

Scoring Seats at Fantasmic

They tell you to arrive an hour before show time to get into this wildly popular show, but, since *everybody* does that, you'll increase your odds if you arrive even earlier.

The Great Movie Ride

Housed in a replica of Mann's Chinese Theater, this ride takes you on a memorable trip through the great movie classics. A tram with a live guide moves you through a multimedia show that includes everything from encounters with the munchkins of *The Wizard of Oz* to a western shoot-out where you're caught in the crossfire between the real and the imaginary. You'll want to ride this one more than once, so you don't miss anything.

Indiana Jones Stunt Spectacular

Re-creating scenes from the action-packed Indiana Jones movies, this riveting and laugh-a-minute show is staged in a 2,200-seat open-air amphitheater. Members of the audience are chosen to participate as extras, while the cast and crew perform awesome stunts—complete with pyrotechnics—and the show's host explains the techniques behind them.

Jim Henson's Muppet Vision 3D

After visiting a reproduction of the Muppets set, watch a funny film featuring the late Henson's winsome stars and some startling 3-D effects. Even if you don't know the difference between the divine Miss Piggie and Babe the Pig, you'll enjoy this one.

The Magic of Disney Animation

This walking tour of a working animation studio is the educational part of your visit to Disney MGM. Here you'll glimpse what Disney does best. Beginning in a gallery that displays Disney's Oscar statuettes and animated clips from Disney classics, the tour describes the animation process with a short film featuring Walter Cronkite and Robin Williams as (pre-taped) guides. Visitors then walk through viewing galleries above the studio where they observe various stages of the animation process of an upcoming Disney movie. The tour ends with a 10-minute film that showcases scenes from Disney's animated hits.

Star Tours

This motion-simulator ride was jointly conceived by Disney's Imagineers and *Star Wars* creator George Lucas. Led by Star Wars droids C3PO and R2D2, travelers board a StarSpeeder for a voyage to the moon of Endor. Considered state-of-the-art when it debuted, Star Tours still delivers a lively ride.

Catastrophe Canyon for the Faint of Heart
Sit inside the car, not in the window seats, if you'd rather not be so close to the pyrotechnics.

Studio Backlot Tour

Aboard a tram, guests snake through the back lots of a working movie and TV studio, past a prop and costume warehouse and a street lined with the facades of houses familiar from the big and small screens. Of course, "something goes terribly wrong" and the tram ends up in **Catastrophe Canyon**, where fire and floods threaten.

Twilight Zone Tower of Terror

At the end of Sunset Boulevard looms the wonderfully decrepit Hollywood Tower Hotel, where guests enter a world of illusion. From the "doo-doo-doo-doo" theme song, to Rod Serling and the holographic eyeball, this thrill ride re-creates the scariest elements of *The Twilight Zone* (a TV classic that aired from 1959–1965). And that's all before the main event, when the service elevator you're standing in plummets 13 stories (even past an open window). No matter how many times you do this ride, it'll always give you a jolt.

Voyage of the Little Mermaid

Worth doing if you've got young kids in tow, this musical stage show is based on the 1989 animated hit *The Little Mermaid*. The production is enhanced by special effects like misty undersea "fog."

SeaWorld Orlando★★★

7007 SeaWorld Dr. From downtown, follow I-4 West to Exit 72, then follow signs to SeaWorld. 407-351-3600 or 800-432-1178. www.seaworldorlando.com. Open year-round daily 9am. Closing times vary, depending on events. $51.95 adults, $42.95 children (ages 3–9).

Recently expanded, this marine adventure park blends entertainment and education in a splashy seaport milieu. Opened in 1973, the park is one of three SeaWorld properties nationwide. Together, these parks, owned by Anheuser-Busch, support the world's largest collection of marine life. Behind the scenes, SeaWorld is actively involved in research and breeding programs, and has successfully bred orca (killer) whales. With its Beached Animal Rescue and Rehabilitation Program, SeaWorld has assisted hundreds of wild creatures in distress, including manatees, dolphins and whales. To the SeaWorld visitor, though, it's all about the rides and shows, especially the wildly popular **Shamu Adventure**.

The major landmark at SeaWorld is the 55ft **lighthouse**, painted with a stylized image of Shamu. (It's no accident that this is where the "lost parents" office is located.) Then there's Sky Tower, a 400ft structure with a bar at its base. Even with these visual cues to guide you, you'll still spend some time walking around in circles with your nose buried in the SeaWorld map. Eventually, though, you'll find your way to Shamu, and most adults somehow manage to locate the Anheuser-Busch Hospitality Center, featuring samples of the company's famous product.

Tips for Visiting

The best strategy for doing SeaWorld is to plan your day around the shows you want to see, and break up all that sitting with tours through **Pacific Point Preserve** (seals and sea lions) and **Penguin Encounter**, and a visit to **Stingray Lagoon**. Add a jolt of adrenalin when you need it with SeaWorld's meanest coaster, **Kraken** (if you dare) and thrill rides **Journey to Atlantis** (a waterfall flume) and **Wild Arctic**. Plan to arrive early at those attractions if you want to stay on schedule—you'll need a game plan if you really want to catch them all!

At the Shamu show an irreverent mime, who is every bit as entertaining as the five-ton headliner of Shamu Adventure, will amuse you while you wait.

Some of the entertainment at SeaWorld takes no planning at all. In the new **Waterfront** area, street-side performers include an old sea captain who tells fish stories, and a band of chefs who make music (sort of) with their pots and pans.

Journey to Atlantis

SeaWorld's flume ride creates the mythical lost city of Atlantis, mysteriously arisen from the floor of the Aegean Sea. You're an explorer aboard a Greek fishing boat, actually a high-speed coaster that carries you through dark passageways haunted by evil sirens. You plummet down a nearly vertical 60ft waterfall and around a pair of S-curves into another free-falling plunge.

Key West at SeaWorld

The most intriguing feature of this quirky little village is **Stingray Lagoon,** where visitors can touch the broad, velvety fish as they swim past. Watching these creatures glide through the pool is truly mesmerizing, and you'll be awestruck by their beauty.

Kraken

Named after a mythical sea monster, screaming yellow Kraken is billed as Orlando's "longest, fastest, tallest, steepest," roller coaster, although those bragging rights will last about fifteen minutes, until somebody builds the next one. Nevertheless, this coaster is truly scary, featuring heights up to 15 stories, speeds of 65mph (while dropping, mind you), and seven upside-down twists.

Manatees: The Last Generation?

Between encounters with powerboats and mysterious viruses, the West Indian manatee lives a perilous existence in its US range in South Florida. Take a peek at the underwater world of the gentle, one-ton sea cow, and you'll come to appreciate this roly-poly, whiskered creature and learn how to protect the species from extinction. SeaWorld operates an ongoing manatee release program, in which orphaned or injured sea cows are nursed to health and reintroduced into the wild.

Nautilus Theater

Debuting at SeaWorld is a brand-new stage show that combines amazing acrobatic feats with special effects and music, set in an underwater fantasy world. This is what SeaWorld does best, so it's bound to be worth a half-hour of your vacation time.

Pacific Point Preserve

The rocky shoals of an open-air pool capture the atmosphere of the Pacific coast. Harbor and fur seals bob in the waters, sea lions lounge on the rocks, and a pinniped symphony of sounds is always in progress.

Penguin Encounter

Step on a moving walkway for a ride past a frosty 30°F setting, where puffins, murres and several species of penguins reside. Watch for a few moments, and you'll start to discern the difference between the king, the gentoo, and the rockhopper penguin. Through a glass-walled observation pool you can see these graceful flightless birds as they swim.

Sea Lion and Otter Stadium

Who knew these creatures could be so entertaining? Sea lions Clyde and Seamore, the Abbott and Costello of the pinniped family, star as stranded buccaneers in Clyde and Seamore Take Pirate Island. After a clever otter steals a pirate's treasure map, he enlists the help of the duo in recovering the wealth. A harbor seal gets into the act, as does a hapless guest, plucked out of the audience. The show's theme changes periodically, but plot really doesn't matter here—it's all about the antics of the stars.

Shamu Stadium

SeaWorld's signature attraction showcases the world's most famous killer whale, five-ton Shamu, and his protégés. Guided by their trainers (who somehow manage to keep smiling even underwater), the whales leap and twirl to music in an amazingly graceful water ballet that is simultaneously captured on an immense high-resolution video screen. Trainers jump right into the pool with the whales, and undertake some equally impressive feats. As a prelude, animal expert Jack Hanna introduces the audience to Alaska's Glacier Bay, the fjords of Norway and the sub-Antarctic Crozet Islands of the South Indian Ocean. Video footage of whales in their natural habitats is enhanced when Shamu and pals exhibit the same behaviors. Avoid the first 14 or so rows if you don't want to be doused with icy salt water—of course, that's precisely where your kids will want to be. *(Arrive 30 minutes before scheduled show time.)*

Theme Parks

Terrors of the Deep

A walk-through shark tank is a must-have at aquariums these days. SeaWorld's version features 600,000 gallons of water, designed to accommodate the swimming patterns of sharks. Five different species of this toothsome predator glide through the water here, along with moray eels, lionfish, barracuda and other denizens of the deep—representing the largest collection of "dangerous sea creatures" in the world, they say. (Next door, there's a restaurant that specializes in seafood.)

Base Station Brrr

It's rather cold in this base station, so don't visit Wild Arctic immediately after doing the water ride Journey to Atlantis. Visitors who don't want to be pitched around on the motion simulator can skip it, and journey to the base station via a gentler, simulated cross-country ski tour.

The Waterfront

SeaWorld's recent addition is a five-acre seaport "village" with new shows, restaurants and shops. Called the Waterfront, the new area features three neighborhoods, called High Street, Harbor Square and Tower Island. On High Street, the main events include **Kit 'n' Kaboodle**, a cat show featuring more than 10 exotic breeds, and a musical revue called **Rico & Roza's Musical Feast**. This, you watch while eating lunch at the new SeaFire Inn (warning: audience participation is encouraged). Harbor Square, at the center of the Waterfront, is the scene of daily performances by the **"Seaport Symphony,"** a band of chefs who make music with pots and pans. Chefs make pizza, not music, at **Voyagers Wood Fired Pizza**, the Waterfront's largest eatery, where they toss the pies skyward—the old-fashioned way. Elsewhere in the park, strolling entertainers include the Harbormaster, the old sea captain, and the Longshoremen, who entertain visitors with street comedy and stunts. On Tower Island, park goers can, as always, ride to the top of **Sky Tower** for lofty views of SeaWorld and environs. And thanks to the new SandBar, you can top off your ride with a frozen drink.

Wild Arctic

A motion-simulator helicopter ride takes passengers on a chilly adventure, pitching and rolling over a frozen landscape dotted with caribou, polar bears and narwhals. After narrowly escaping an avalanche and dodging chunks of iceberg, you disembark at a mock research station in the Arctic. Here, you stroll past tanks with above- and below-water views of beluga whales, polar bears, walruses and harbor seals.

Discovery Cove★★

6000 Discovery Way (International Dr.). Adjacent to SeaWorld. Reservations required (4–6 weeks in advance advised); admission limited to 1,000 visitors/day. 877-434-7268. www.discoverycove.com. Open year-round daily 8:30am–5:30pm. Three packages available: $229 all-inclusive, $129 non-dolphin swim, and $399 trainer-for-a-day.

If your list of "Things I Want to Do Before I Die" includes "swim with dolphins," here's your chance to make it happen. At around $200 per person, this fantasy won't come cheap, but then, neither will "hiking Mt. Everest." (To sweeten the deal, they throw in an admission pass good for seven consecutive days at SeaWorld.)

And If I Don't Want A Dolphin Encounter?

Guests who choose not to swim with dolphins can enjoy the rest of the park, for about half the cost of the dolphin encounter. Masks, snorkels, towels and beach chairs are provided. Nix the sunscreen—the park provides a specially formulated one that is safe for use in animal habitats. Discovery Cove promotes itself as a place to spend a full day. Lunch is included in the package.

If it happens to be a bit chilly on the day you visit—and those days do happen in Orlando—they'll provide you with a wetsuit. No matter what the weather, the water temperature is always 78–85°F.

This 30-acre marine park, owned by Busch Entertainment Corp., SeaWorld's parent company, comprises a series of pools and lagoons set amidst sandy beaches. Adding to the tropical environment are towering palm trees and thatched huts.

What Else Is There To Do?

- Snorkel through a "coral reef" with exotic fish and several grottoes, even a submerged shipwreck.
- Feed the birds inside a net-enclosed aviary that contains some 300 tropical birds in free flight.
- Snorkel through **Ray Lagoon**, where you can touch, feed and interact with cownose and southern rays up to 4ft in diameter. (Snorkeling lessons are offered at no additional cost.)
- Float on an inner tube down the river that runs through the park, past waterfalls and lush greenery.
- Relax on the beach, or paddle around in the swimming lagoon.

Discovery Cove Highlights

For most guests, the lure of **swimming with the dolphins** is too enticing to resist. Children are especially captivated by these sleek, gentle animals *(children must be at least 6 years old to participate in the dolphin swim)*. The entire experience lasts about 45 minutes. Guests are first briefed on the behavior and physique of the dolphin, as well as given general rules for the swim experience. After a brief orientation film, swimmers enter the water in small groups to become acquainted, one on one, with one of the 30 or so dolphins in the group. Adult dolphins average 8–10ft and weigh 300–600 pounds. Next comes the major highlight of the experience—a ride on the dolphin. This is perfectly safe for the animal, they say, as long as the rider doesn't place hands on or near the mammal's blowhole. If you're really blown away by this experience, consider signing up for the Trainer for a Day program; this gives you eight hours alongside experts to train and care for a dolphin, anteater, birds, or other animals. Plus, they throw in a dolphin swim.

Should I Feel OK About This?

Of course, responsible animal lovers want to know if they should take part in this kind of activity. Some of the swim-with-dolphin programs offered elsewhere have gotten a bad rap due to their treatment of the animals. Regarding Discovery Cove, the SeaWorld philosophy of protecting the animals applies: The more people experience animals, the more they will help protect and preserve them. Discovery Cove's "animal ambassador," Julie Scardina, also points out that Discovery Cove has assembled an expert staff of animal trainers to work with guests, and that the habitats at the park are specially designed to encourage personal interaction between animals and people. Habitats also provide animals with the freedom to move away from the action for a while, if they choose to. Beyond that, all of the dolphins at Discovery Cove have been specially selected and trained for guest interaction. The training process is based on positive reinforcement and maintaining a relationship of mutual trust and respect. Many of the dolphins at Discovery Cove are not wild, but are the product of SeaWorld's breeding program. Ultimately, it's your call.

Universal Orlando★★★

1000 Universal Studios Plaza. Follow I-4 West to Exit 74. Turn right on Hollywood Way and follow signs to Universal Studios. 407-363-8000. www.universalorlando.com. Open year-round daily 9am. Closing times may vary depending upon events. $51.95 adults, $42.95 children (ages 3–9).

If you want to go head-to-head with Disney, you need to bring out the big guns. And that's what Universal Studios did, when they opened their first Florida attraction in 1990. With Steven Spielberg as a creative consultant, how could they go wrong? This 444-acre theme park and working studio ranks as the largest motion picture and television facility outside Hollywood. Intended as a place where visitors can "ride the movies," the park bases its attractions on popular films and television shows. This continues the tradition begun in 1915 by the studio's founder, Carl Laemmle, who encouraged paying visitors to stop by and watch movies being made at his movie studio outside Los Angeles.

Universal Studios' arrival not only gave Orlando vacationers yet another place to play, it also upped the ante on thrill rides and attractions— the rides at Universal Orlando really *rock*. With the latest state-of-the-art amusement

> **Lay of the Land**
> While the Disney parks are spread out over dozens of square miles of former orange groves, Universal's property is much more compact, even after a major expansion in 1999 that included a new theme park, **Islands of Adventure**, and a dining, entertainment and shopping complex, **Universal CityWalk**. Major "theme hotels" have been added to the mix as well, sited close enough to the parks so guests can walk or take a boat ride to entrance gates.

technology, Universal pushed the envelope, offering special effects that dazzled and defied the imagination. These days, Universal manages to keep all their old favorites going—like **E.T. Adventure, Jaws**, and **Terminator 2: 3-D**, while adding new attractions like **Men in Black Alien Attack**, **Shrek 4-D** and **Revenge of the Mummy**.

Universal takes a hip, irreverent tone with its content. Laced with insider jokes and irony, you get the feeling they don't take this stuff too seriously. The streets of Universal Orlando's re-created New York, for example, are rather more decrepit than Disney-MGM's. Another difference here is the population of celebrity look-alikes, who pose for photos with visitors (think Marilyn, not Mickey).

A brass band and the Blues Brothers provide street theater, although you never know who will show up. Chrome and glass-block shops and eateries line the Front Lot, where Laurel and Hardy or Charlie Chaplin look-alikes might put in an appearance. Universal's reproduction of Hollywood delivers legendary landmarks such as the Beverly Wilshire Hotel and Schwab's Soda Fountain. Among replicas of the exclusive storefronts of Rodeo Drive lies **Lucy, A Tribute**, a gallery devoted to actress-comedienne Lucille Ball, with memora-bilia and clips from the *I Love Lucy* show. Other "neighborhoods" include San Francisco, marked with the old Ghirardelli chocolate factory and Fisherman's Wharf, and Amity, the fictional setting of the 1975 movie hit *Jaws*. With its weathered clapboard facades, this New England seaside motif looks like Mar-tha's Vineyard (where *Jaws* was actually filmed).

Since streets sometimes double as movie sets at Universal, you might see a film in progress as you tour the park. You may also visit soundstages such as the one used full-time by television's Nickelodeon Network. While there are some live shows sprinkled in the mix, Universal Orlando is really all about the rides. And the great thing about Universal is, adults get as much of a kick out of it as youngsters do. For every E.T. Adventure, there's a Mummy's Revenge. And of course they've got first dibs on all the hottest Nicktoon characters like

When in San Francisco . . .

The best quick, cheap eats at Universal Orlando are in "San Francisco," at the re-created Fisherman's Wharf area. Here you can get an ample serving of chowder in an edible sourdough bread bowl.

SpongeBob SquarePants, Hey Arnold, and The Fairly OddParents (all make cameos at **Jimmy Neutron's Nicktoon Blast**). Once your kids graduate from Nickelodeon to MTV and grow tall enough to ride coasters, though, *nothing* is going to keep them from **Islands of Adventure**, where the big kids play.

UNIVERSAL HIGHLIGHTS

Animal Planet Live

You don't need to be owned by a pet to appreciate this show, where the screen's most lovable animal stars—Lassie, Beethoven, Mister Ed—perform tricks with a live supporting cast of cats, birds and other animals.

Back to the Future: The Ride

In Universal's most popular ride, you'll heed the taped plea of Doc Brown (actor Christopher Lloyd) to help save the universe from the evil villain Biff Tannen. Board a Time Vehicle (a DeLorean to you and me) for a white-knuckle flight into the Ice Age, where you'll thunder over glacial fields and free-fall into a flaming volcano. Multisensory special effects enhance the "wow" factor.

Beetlejuice's Graveyard Revue

The kids will have no idea who Beetlejuice is, but no matter. They'll still enjoy this campy romp, featuring the headliner, Dracula, Frankenstein and the missus, and other movie monsters, who stomp their way through rock-'n-roll classics.

Tips for Visiting

Universal has instituted an **Express Pass** system for reserving ride times at the most popular attractions (get a pass inside the park or present your room key at the ride entrance if you're staying at Universal).

Other strategies for reducing wait times: Arrive 30min–1hr prior to the park's opening time. As soon as gates open, head for **The Mummy**, **Shrek 4-D** or **Men in Black Alien Attack**, then visit **Twister**, **Terminator 2: 3-D**, **Back to the Future** and **JAWS**. Follow up with **E.T. Adventure** and **FUNtastic World of Hanna-Barbera**. Plan to catch the shows during midday, when ride lines are longest (check the Preview of Today's Rides and Shows for times). Or sign up for the **VIP Tour Experience**, which gives you priority entrance (they sneak you in) to leading attractions (reservations: 407-363-8295).

Earthquake: The Big One

After a behind-the-scenes peek at how Charlton Heston made the movie *Earthquake* in 1974, visitors board a San Francisco subway car for a truly groundbreaking trip—in which the earth moves and cataclysm follows.

E.T. Adventure

The magic of Steven Spielberg's classic film is captured here, where waiting lines weave through a dark, dreamy Northwest forest, scented with evergreens. E.T. has returned to Earth to obtain our assistance in healing his Green Planet, which has fallen ill. Riders hop aboard bicycles that carry them and the adorable extraterrestrial on an airborne adventure toward E.T.'s beloved home.

The FUNtastic World of Hanna-Barbera

Don't be fooled by the cartoony theme; this one ranks as one of the park's most action-packed rides. Strapped into your seat, you'll take a simulated zoom through cartoonland, visiting the Flintstones, the Jetsons, Yogi Bear and a host of other Hanna-Barbera favorites along the way. The exit leads into a hands-on playroom filled with cartoon whimsy. (For those interested in the cartoon but not the motion, stationary seats are located in the front of the theater.)

JAWS

On a cruise through the waters off Amity, passengers find themselves virtually in the maw of that infamous, indestructible Great White Shark. Boat pilots, however, have a few tricks up their sleeves, and after some spectacular fiery clashes, all are returned safely to shore. Up close, the shark looks like a giant rubber pool toy, but that won't stop you from enjoying the ride.

Men in Black Alien Attack

OK, so it's really just a ramped-up version of laser tag. Still, this ride is the first in history to allow two side-by-side vehicles to compete in this activity, with tabulated scores visible in each car. Riding in "training vehicles," passengers aim "alien zappers" at some 120 electronic targets that pop up along the route. Computerization generates a choice of 12 different ride endings and thousands of ride experience options.

Nickelodeon Studios Tour

This tour offers visitors a look at the two soundstages used by Nickelodeon. Even when the cameras aren't rolling, a guide explains the process of putting a show together and leads guests past soundstages, make-up and hair departments, and dressing rooms.

Revenge of the Mummy

Based on the popular "Mummy" films starring Brendan Fraser, this indoor thrill ride was ten years in the making. If you liked the creepy effects in those movies—flesh melting on skulls, scarab beetles oozing out of pyramids—you'll love this one, conceived by "Mummy" series director Stephen Sommers. It's a high-speed coaster that propels riders through ancient Egyptian catacombs amid wild pyrotechnical effects, including a "ceiling of flame." Producers spent many hours at the British Museum to get the ride's shadowy, curse-ridden interior propped just right, complete with dusty canopic jars containing the grisly remains of long-deceased royalty. Beware: You never know who might leap from the netherworld tomb and into your vehicle.

Shrek 4-D

To know Shrek is to love him, and this 3-D film/special-effects show picks up where the Oscar-winning movie left off. Join the jolly green ogre, Shrek, and Princess Fiona on their honeymoon. Wearing 3-D glasses, you take in all the action (the happy couple doesn't sit around drinking Mai-Tais on the beach) and you feel the action as well, right from your seat. Even if you didn't see *Shrek*, you'll find this movie—enhanced with the miracle of OgreVision—a hoot.

Terminator 2: 3-D

Arnold's back with a vengeance in this attraction based on the hit movies. The gripping 12min film marries stunt work, state-of-the-art special effects and in-your-face 3-D to keep viewers on the edge of their seats.

Twister! Ride it Out

A take-off on the 1996 blockbuster movie of the same name, Twister! subjects you to the fury of a large tornado as it rages through a rural town on the Great Plains. You're right in the thick of the chaos, near broken water mains, tanker fires and, of course, that famous flying cow.

Wild, Wild Wild West Stunt Show

Commandeering the stage of an amphitheater, the Clod Hopper clan hams it up with fancy shootin' and stunts.

Universal's Islands of Adventure★★★

1000 Universal Studios Plaza. Follow I-4 West to Exit 74. Turn right on Hollywood Way and follow signs to Islands of Adventure. 407-363-8000. www.universalorlando.com. Open year-round daily 9am. Closing times vary depending upon events. $51.95 adults, $42.95 children (ages 3–9).

Over-the-top design, stomach-churning rides, and wonderful diversions for the small fry—this park has it all. With producer-director Steven Spielberg as creative consultant, "Islands," unveiled in 1999, is recognized industry-wide as a triumph of imagination. Swooping roller-coaster loops soar sky-high over this high-tech amusement complex, above five themed "islands." The **Port of Entry** commercial area serves as the departure point for Universal Orlando's man-made archipelago around a large lagoon. **Seuss Landing** features cartoon-like architecture and whimsical characters straight out of Theodor "Dr. Seuss" Geisel's madcap children's books. Meanwhile, **Toon Lagoon** brings classic cartoon characters to life, while **Jurassic Park** is populated with realistic dinosaurs. Thrill rides are the main attractions at **The Lost Continent,** based on fantasy novels and movies. But just when you think rides couldn't get any wilder than **Dueling Dragons**, wander over to **Marvel Super Hero Island.** Here the way-cool **Amazing Adventures of Spider-Man** and the **Incredible Hulk Coaster** supply enough adrenalin rush to get you through the next day or two—and certainly through a late night of clubbing at **Universal CityWalk**!

> **Port of Entry**
> The park's starting point is laid out like a port town, with a looming lighthouse and bustling arcade of food and beverage outlets, like **Backwater Bar**. Most visitors stop at shops like **Ocean Trader Market**, on their way out, not in, as you would suspect. And lest you forget you're in a theme park, there's **Betty Boop**, hanging with . . . **Popeye**? There seems to be a bit of intermingling among island characters here, but that just adds to the offbeat charm of the place.

JURASSIC PARK

This island re-creates the creepy dinosaurs-run-amok motif from the moment you pass under the archway. Although the dinosaur theme has been done to death—even Disney does it at Animal Kingdom—the rides will win you over, an interesting juxtaposition of really cute and really scary.

Jurassic Park River Adventure

Part flume ride, part scary fun-house, this ride is quick and nasty. The gist of it is, you're pursued by a realistic *Tyrannosaurus rex* with mayhem on its mind. We won't spoil the surprise, but we will tell you that the only escape is down an 85ft water chute—supposedly, the longest, steepest and fastest built to date.

Pteranodon Flyers

Got a small child, or a tiny adult in your party? One of you has to be 52in tall or shorter in order to glide in these two-person gondolas, which suspend from a curving track. The convey-ances look like ancient flying creatures with 10ft wings—very cool—and they fly over Camp Jurassic, with its volcano and amber mine.

THE LOST CONTINENT

Dominated by the hills and valleys of the Dueling Dragons coaster, this fantasy island sports a medieval motif. Shops specialize in pointy princess hats and fake swords, but the **Enchanted Oak Tavern and Alchemy Bar** really gets the theme down pat: it's shaped like an enormous, gnarly oak tree and serves Viking-worthy turkey legs and tall tankards of ale. What parent *wouldn't* be tempted to hunker down here while waiting for the kids to do Dueling Dragons?

Dueling Dragons

A must-ride for coaster enthusiasts, too terrifying to contemplate for normal folk, Dueling Dragons ups the danger quotient with two zooming coaster cars on a collision course. As if that's not scary enough, the coaster is inverted, with two intertwined tracks, so your legs dangle freely. Riders climb, four abreast, onto a dragon representing Fire or Ice. As the two dragons shoot through a medieval forest, they climb 125ft, side-by-side. Then, Fire shoots off to the left at 60mph and Ice dives right to complete a series of upside-down flips that involve near-misses with one another.

> ### Triceratops Encounter? No Thanks
>
> More of a lowlight than a highlight, put Triceratops Encounter on your "mustn't see" list—unless you like the idea of walking and walking, and waiting and waiting, for the dubious pleasure of watching a life-like dinosaur urinate.

Eighth Voyage of Sinbad

After Dueling Dragons, you'll appreciate a ride where you can sit back and watch other people perform daredevil feats. Legendary Sinbad sets out on a death-defying voyage, dodging water explosions and all manner of fiery dangers, in-cluding a 10ft-high circle of flames. The plot is kind of vague, but visual overload, not story line, is the main point here.

MARVEL SUPER HERO ISLAND

This island is a favorite with fearless older kids and coaster-crazed adults—it's the home of the **Incredible Hulk Coaster** and a very hairy ride, **Amazing Adventures of Spider-Man**. Beyond those must-dos, there's **Captain Marvel's Diner**, a fairly inexpensive choice for refreshments, and a complement of characters, including **Spider-Man**, **The X-Men**, and **Doctor Doom**.

Amazing Adventures of Spider-Man

This one is a theme-park first, they say: an attraction that combines moving vehicles, filmed 3-D action and special effects. You'll wait in a seemingly endless line for the privilege of experiencing this, but it really is amazing. As passengers try to help Spider-Man retrieve the stolen Statue of Liberty, they don 3-D night-sight goggles, take a 400ft "sensory drop" into darkness, and speed around a 1.5-acre set loaded with fiery battles between good and evil.

> **Spider-Man, the Wimpy Way**
>
> Finding the whole Spider-Man thing a little too intense? Discreetly take off those 3-D goggles—though it's only *slightly* tamer that way.

Doctor Doom's Fearfall

Squeeze this one in *before* you dine at Captain Marvel's. One of those elevator-type rides, this one rockets you 150ft into the air, then pushes you back down faster than gravity.

Incredible Hulk Coaster

Which one is better, Dueling Dragons or the Hulk? Each has its fans, but both offer thrills aplenty. Here, passengers are shot out of Dr. Banner's Gamma Force Accelerator with the same G-force as an F-16 jet. They zoom from 0 to 40mph in 2 seconds, roll over 7 times in a series of chilling swoops and loops, and plunge underground twice, all within a time frame of just over 2 minutes.

SEUSS LANDING

Like stepping into a Dr. Seuss book, this island's architecture lacks symmetry and straight lines. Mounts on the elaborate **Caro-Seuss-el** are all Seussian creations—no pretty ponies here. For refreshments, dine at the **Green Eggs and Ham Café**, where the eggs are actually green, or sip slurpies at **Moose Juice Goose Juice**. Shops sell all the books, of course, along with stuffed Cat-in-the-Hats and Grinches, and the must-have floppy striped hat.

The Cat in the Hat

Ride on 6-passenger couches through 18 scenes from Seuss books, including a 24ft, perception-altering tunnel. Some 30 Seuss characters join the fun, among them the Cat in the Hat.

One Fish, Two Fish, Red Fish, Blue Fish

On this one, you ride a fish, steering it to avoid squirts from a series of waterspouts and streams. All the while, a rhyming riddle is broadcast to give clues on how to stay dry while rising and dropping 15ft within the orbit.

> **Photo Ops at Seuss Landing**
>
> Look for the Grinch, Thing 1 and Thing 2, and other Seuss characters, in front of **Dr. Seuss' All the Books You Can Read** (at 11am, 2pm & 4pm). Pose for a picture with the Grinch if you dare; he's pleasantly nasty, and may well put a hairy green hand in front of your tot's face when you snap the shutter.

TOON LAGOON

On this colorful isle, comic books and cartoons come to life, especially along **Comic Strip Lane**, home of the Pandemonium Cartoon Circus. There's a great photo op here, too; look for the giant-sized Little Orphan Annie comic, where you can poke your head in and become part of the strip. And if there's one place to eat an overstuffed sandwich, it's at **Blondie's: Home of the Dagwood Sandwich**, where you pay according to the thickness of the sandwich you construct.

Dudley Do-Right's Ripsaw Falls

Nell's in trouble, and the bumbling Canadian Mountie of *Rocky and Bullwinkle* fame must save her from the evil Snidely Whiplash. Visitors join the rescue, which ends with a 15ft plunge beneath the surface of a lagoon, the first-ever ride below water level. Count on getting wet.

Popeye and Bluto's Bilge-Rat Barges

The 12 passengers on this surging white-water raft ride get squirted by a water cannon from Popeye's boat and encounter an 18ft octopus, its 12ft tentacles bulging with water. In case you didn't get wet enough, the boat goes through a "boat wash" at the end.

You've paid oodles of money and waited in endless lines—for what? For the privilege of being scared witless on a coaster, or being plunged into a blow-your-mind, imaginary world dreamed up by techno-nerds, that's what! Might as well make the most of it. Here's the hot list, featuring the cutest of the cute, the baddest of the bad, and the best of all the rest.

MAGIC KINGDOM

407-939-7600. www.disneyworld.com.

Big Thunder Mountain Railroad

Remember when roller coasters clicked and clacked on wooden tracks before that pregnant pause, when they went—big squeals here—barreling *straight down*? This one still does, and the ramshackle look of it all boosts the fear factor.

Buzz Lightyear's Space Ranger Spin

Climb aboard a space shuttle, travel the galaxy and shoot stuff—what could be more America-and-apple pie than this? You get points for every target you hit, so it's highly addictive; look out for over-stimulated dads trying to cut in line.

It's a Small World

Top marks for nostalgia go to this little boat ride, where it's all Peace, Love and Harmony, and everybody on the planet is two feet tall and sings the same sappy song.

Peter Pan's Flight

If this ride were invented today, they'd have you actually flying through London holding Pete's hand. But considering the fact that it's more than 30 years old, Peter Pan's Flight can still hold its own in the visual-wonder department.

Pirates of the Caribbean

Oh-so politically incorrect, you've just got to love it! These disheveled old salts swill rum, chase women, and raise havoc in a very un-Disney-like fashion. This ride would never get made today, which is precisely the reason Disney had better not touch it. (The moth-eaten bandannas only add to its appeal.)

Snow White's Adventures

Can a kiddie ride be scary? You betcha. Happily, they've re-tuned this one down a bit, so the focus is more on the lovely Snow White, less on the mean witch with the poisoned apple.

Space Mountain

Space Mountain set the standard for Disney thrill rides years ago, when this coaster first plunged into the black hole of eternity. This is where everyone sprints to when the park first opens. Space Mountain's fan base is almost cult-like; folks ride it over and over again, visit after visit. Compare that to the much newer Alien Encounter, which you only need to do once. You haven't done Disney if you haven't done Space Mountain, so do it even if you're not a coaster person—it's such a smooth ride, it's actually easier on the stomach than rickety Big Thunder Mountain.

EPCOT

407-939-7600. www.disneyworld.com.

El Rio del Tiempo (World Showcase Mexico)

This languid boat-ride-through-time is a great treat when you're hot, cranky and suffering from Epcot overload. (It's even kind of romantic.) Stick around and have lunch afterwards at the dimly-lit San Angel Inn Restaurant.

Maelstrom (World Showcase Norway)

On a sweltering Orlando day, even the idea of Scandinavia might be enough to cool you down. While you're there (deciding you're not really in the mood for the smorgasbord's creamed herring after all), board a dragon-headed longboat (inspired by the actual vessels used by the Vikings) and take a scenic cruise through Norway via the stormy North Sea. Uh-oh—look out for troublesome trolls as you travel!

Mission: SPACE

Indulge your astronaut fantasies here, where four guests become a team of space cadets, working together to fulfill a mission. You enter a space capsule and prepare for lift-off (and a pulse-racing sensation it is), blasting off into outer space. Everyone in the capsule participates, by using joysticks and buttons, and viewing outer space through the window (OK, video screen). All this is set in a sleek metallic space station, with planetary orbs and a 12ft moon.

Test Track

The attraction that put Epcot back on the map, Test Track is one of the most expensive rides ever built by Disney. Where else can you slam your car into a wall (well, sort of) and walk away without an increase in your insurance premium? Plus, you can drive 65mph—try doing *that* anyplace else in traffic-clogged Orlando!

DISNEY'S ANIMAL KINGDOM

407-939-7600. www.disneyworld.com.

Dinosaur

It isn't a day at the park if you don't go on at least one spine-jarring motion simulator ride. This one takes you to the late-Cretaceous period to bring home a living dinosaur and save the planet from a giant asteroid.

Kilimanjaro Safaris

This faux-African safari is the best thing going at Animal Kingdom. Suspend belief for a few moments and you'll swear you're in Kenya, chugging down a rutted road in search of big game. You'll see it, too. This is the real thing, not animated, pop-up versions of same. They could have left it at that, but this is a theme park, so there's the requisite chase, bad guys, and generally corny plot, all (of course) with a happy ending. Ride it again, at a different time of day, and you may see a different cast of (animal) characters.

Primeval Whirl

It's billed as a kiddie coaster but nobody will kick you off if you're not a member of the Happy Meal set. Ride. Enjoy. Squeal like a 12-year-old.

DISNEY MGM STUDIOS

407-939-7600. www.disneyworld.com.

Aerosmith's Rock 'n' Roller Coaster

Stratocasters in the stratosphere? Not that you'll notice. You'll be *way* too busy trying not to lose your lunch as you fly through Hollywood in an out-of-control limo set to the hard-rock rhythms of Aerosmith.

The Great Movie Ride

The must-do ride at Disney MGM is a time-travel tram trip through movie history. Even the original *Alien* is part of the action.

Star Tours

Re-live the fun of seeing *Star Wars* for the first time on this motion-simulator ride—also a classic. R2D2 and C3PO pilot your StarSpeeder to a galaxy far, far away.

Twilight Zone Tower of Terror

Everybody's nightmare, the plunging elevator, is the concept here, where the fear factor is heightened by the creepy set design and Rod Serling's cameo appearance. You'll think it's all an illusion, 'til you drop past an open window, and your stomach drops to your kneecaps.

SEAWORLD ORLANDO

407-351-3600. www.seaworldorlando.com.

Kraken

Scary just to look at, never mind ride, SeaWorld's sole roller coaster looms up to 15 stories and turns you upside down seven—count 'em!—times.

Wild Arctic

On this motion-simulator helicopter ride, you ride, herky-jerky, past polar bears and icebergs and dodge an avalanche. Once you exit, though, the adventure continues as you stroll past real polar bears, narwhals, beluga whales, and other Arctic critters on exhibit. Just when you think you're headed outdoors, you're disgorged into—guess what?—a gift shop.

UNIVERSAL ORLANDO

407-363-8000. www.universalorlando.com.

Back to the Future: The Ride

So this is what happened to those unsold DeLoreans! Universal's most popular ride delivers awesome special effects, if a rather sketchy story line.

E.T. Adventure

This impossibly cute, dreamlike ride re-creates the magic of the movie. You're transported on a bicycle with a basket, and . . . well, we don't want to spoil the surprise. Adults love it as much as—if not more—than kids do.

FUNtastic World of Hanna-Barbera

More exciting than the name implies, this motion-simulator ride takes you on a time-travel trip through cartoonland as remembered by the Baby Boom crowd. Think Yogi and Boo-Boo, the Flintstones, the Jetsons.

JAWS

It's amazing how scary a three-ton, latex-covered fish can be! On this classic ride, you'll cruise through the waters off "Amity," waiting to be shark bait. Even though it's all obviously fake, the suspense builds (maybe it's the *Jaws* theme song that everybody's reacting to) and the payoff will make you jump like a spawning salmon.

Men in Black Alien Attack

Even if you're a lousy shot, you'll have a hoot trying to zap yucky aliens from a moving vehicle. You'll hurtle through the streets of New York City, dodging laser-wielding aliens and potholes and trying to out-shoot the car next to you, until things take a turn for the worse.

Revenge of the Mummy

Inspired by the *Mummy* remakes, this high-speed indoor coaster propels riders through ancient Egyptian catacombs, with lots of creepy encounters and fiery effects along the way. The set design is so amazing, you'll wish you could do Mummy at half-speed to take in all the details. Scariest part: Hoping your hair doesn't catch fire.

UNIVERSAL'S ISLANDS OF ADVENTURE

407-363-8000. www.universalorlando.com.

Amazing Adventures of Spider-Man

Universal designers have managed to put all their gee-whizziest special effects together here, for one amazing ride. It helps to know the Spider-Man comics cast of characters to get the story line, but everything happens so fast, the plot is irrelevant. Count on being bombarded with sensory effects, right up to the point where Doc Ock takes aim at you with his anti-gravity gun and you plummet—or you *think* you do—400ft.

The Cat in the Hat

Sitting on a moving couch, you ride through scenes from Dr. Seuss books. It's almost as much fun as actually meeting the Grinch (psst, he hangs out in front of the bookstore).

Dudley Do-Right's Ripsaw Falls

Every bit as wet as Jurassic Park River Adventure, but this time, the bad guy is Snidely Whiplash, not *Tyrannosaurus rex*. And this time, you go underwater.

Dueling Dragons

On this inverted super-coaster, riders board a dragon representing Fire or Ice and careen through a medieval forest. The cars zoom left and right, and execute a series of loop-de-loops, whipping so close to one another, you're sure you can hear a sickening crunch of steel against steel.

Incredible Hulk Coaster

Think of it as a roller coaster on steroids. You'll be shot upward 10 stories with the same G-force as an F-16 jet, then whipped upside-down, plunged under a bridge, and more or less turned inside out until the whole thing is over—when you'll want to do it again.

Jurassic Park River Adventure

At Universal's replica of Jurassic Park, it's hard to tell what's scary and what's tame just by looking. This one *looks* like an easy-going flume ride—but it's *not*. Unbelievably real-looking dinosaurs, some five stories tall, ratchet up the fright level here, and that's *before* you take an 85ft plunge into the water.

Pteranodon Flyers

Kids can make like prehistoric flying reptiles here, by zipping along in winged gondolas suspended from a track. It's so enchanting, you'll be jealous. Snap a photo as they flutter above you, over Camp Jurassic.

So they're not thrill rides. Even so, these theme-park shows and 3-D movies are ones you shouldn't miss.

Indiana Jones Stunt Spectacular

At Disney MGM Studios. 407-939-7600. www.disneyworld.com.

Who needs Fantasmic!, when you can see real (stunt) people throw fake punches and make things explode?

It's Tough to Be a Bug

At Animal Kingdom. 407-939-7600. www.disneyworld.com.

This "special effects show" sounds adorable, 'til the giant insects come lunging at you! Even 3-D glasses can't protect you from stinkbug emissions and pesticide sprays—you just sit there and take it, laughing all the while.

Kit 'n' Kaboodle

At SeaWorld. 407-351-3600. www.seaworld.com.

Performing cats? Who knew felines would actually do stuff? See it just for the sake of curiosity.

Shamu Show

At SeaWorld. 407-351-3600. www.seaworld.com.

As if you'd miss Shamu and company hurling their massive bodies out of the water and then diving back into the pool! Actually, you might, if you don't get to Shamu Stadium early. Avoid the first 14 rows if you'd rather not drench your camera gear in saltwater.

Tarzan Rocks!

At Animal Kingdom. 407-939-7600. www.disneyworld.com.

What are in-line skaters doing hanging in the jungle with tanned Tarzan and gal-pal Jane? Who knows? But it makes a rollicking good show, appreciated even by the hyper-critical pre-teen crowd.

Terminator 2: 3-D

At Universal Studios Orlando. 407-363-8000. www.universalorlando.com.

Live action and special effects come together here for one outrageous outing. Wait 'til you see the live-action doubles of Ahhnold and Edward Furlong roar onto the stage on Harleys.

Y ou might think the real spectacle occurs when several thousand people go lunging at the gates when the theme parks open—Orlando's less-elegant version of the running of the bulls at Pamplona. Beyond that (unavoidable) spectacle, there are a gazillion parades and fireworks displays at the theme parks alone, plus some terrific shows that should be on every visitor's "To-Do" list. Here are the best picks of the lot.

Arabian Nights

6225 W. Hwy. 192, Kissimmee. 407-239-9223. www.arabian-nights.com.

Orlando offers a slew of dinner-theater options. This is the one to see. The food is just so-so (of course), but the entertainment is an extravagant spectacle of Vegas-worthy costumes and thrilling horseback riding—even chariot races—in a huge indoor equestrian arena.

Cirque du Soleil

At Downtown Disney. 407-939-7600. www.disneyworld.com.

This over-the-top theatrical fantasy features outrageous costumes, high-flying wire and trapeze acts, and extraordinary gymnastics and acrobatics. (How do they do those amazing 360-degree spins while perched on a 90ft-long wire?) Add dazzling sets and a surreal story line and you've got a worthwhile splurge. This troupe of Cirque du Soleil makes its permanent home here.

Dolly Parton's Dixie Stampede

8251 Vineland Ave. 407-238-4455 or 877-782-6733. www.dixiestampede.com.

Don your cowboy boots and straw hats. This down-home dinner show is so hokey, you can't help but laugh. Thirty-two horses, a cast of characters, a slew of country folk musicians and a gaggle of ostriches (yes, you read that right) fill a giant 35,000sq ft arena, designed specifically for Dolly's popular show. There's a minor North versus South plot line, and a four-course, southern-style dinner (think barbecued pork and chicken, corn on the cob and hot biscuits). It all ends with a rah-rah salute to America that invariably brings the crowd to its feet in true, rousing God Bless America form. Pure G-rated family entertainment. Reservations must be made at least seven days in advance.

Fantasmic!

At Disney MGM Studios. 407-824-4321. www.disneyworld.com.

This wildly popular show is a nightly spectacle of lights, lasers, and water effects. Starring (who else?) Disney characters and set to classic Disney tunes, it lasts about 25 minutes—not counting the hour or more you'll wait in line to snag a seat in the amphitheater. Too loud for little ones—they'll much prefer the Magic Kingdom's SpectroMagic Parade if they're staying up late—but a lively ending to a day at the park for everyone else.

SpectroMagic Parade

At Magic Kingdom. 407-824-4321. www.disneyworld.com.

If you can manage to stick around the Magic Kingdom 'til dark, there's a bonus. During evenings in peak periods (*summer & Dec holidays*), the SpectroMagic Parade fills the streets with a dazzling display of Disney characters. The procession walks the 3.4mi Main Street parade route, and features giant Disney superstars outlined in glittery lights. Highlights of this one include way-cool glowing butterflies, and Sorcerer Mickey, with a crystal ball filled with 100 tiny lightning bolts. The parade is often followed by **Fantasy in the Sky**, featuring a flying Tinkerbell and a fireworks display. Don't count on getting too close to the action, unless you sleuth out your spot an hour or two early (try getting a spot in Frontier Land).

Yes, there's an afternoon *(3pm)* procession, too, the **Share A Dream Come True Parade**, but it's not as spectacular. The afternoon parade features giant snow globes filled with Disney characters. (If you visited Mickey's Toontown Fair, you've already seen these guys.) The best strategy is to skip the Share A Dream parade, and ride your favorite rides while *everybody else* watches it.

Best Seats in the House

If you'd rather ditch the SpectroMagic Parade and focus on the Magic Kingdom's fireworks, you'll get great views from the window seats at the California Grill at Disney's Contemporary Resort. (The food's not bad, either.)

House of Blues Gospel Brunch

At Downtown Disney. 407-934-2583. www.disneyworld.com.

Hallelujah and pass the jambalaya. You'll feast on a southern-style BBQ buffet (leave room for the awesome bread pudding in bourbon sauce), then enjoy rousing, live gospel music, performed by talented choruses from around the South. Put your hands together, stomp your feet, and get a feel-good thing going that will last all day.

Think Orlando is all about theme parks? There's more to art than the "Art of Disney" (an actual shop at Disney Village Marketplace), and more to science than . . . well, you get the idea. Here are some worthwhile places to escape the vacationing hordes (not to mention the heat) and expand your mind a bit.

Charles Hosmer Morse Museum of American Art★

5mi north of downtown Orlando in Winter Park. Take I-4 North to Exit 87 (Fairbanks Ave.) Go east on Fairbanks to Park Ave. Turn left onto Park Ave. Museum is at 445 N. Park Ave. 407-645-5311. www.morsemuseum.org. Open year-round Tue–Sat 9:30am–4pm, Sun 1pm– 4pm. Closed Jan 1, Thanksgiving Day & Dec 25. $3.

If you're a fan of stained glass, you'll revel in this extensive group of works from the studios of artist **Louis Comfort Tiffany** (1848–1933). Tiffany's glass forms the centerpiece of the museum's 4,000-piece collection of late 19C and early 20C American and European paintings, decorative and graphic arts, American art pottery, Art Nouveau jewelry and Arts and Crafts furniture. Highlights include the stunning **Magnolia Window** from the Tiffany family's New York City mansion, as well as glass panels by William Morris, Frank Lloyd Wright and John Lafarge.

Founder Jeannette McKean named the museum after her industrialist grandfather, who retired in Winter Park.

Scenic Stroll

To see more of Tiffany's work, stroll to the south end of Park Avenue to the entrance of **Rollins College** *(at Holt Ave.; www.rollins.edu)*, a private, four-year coeducational liberal arts college (established in 1895) located on the shores of Lake Virginia. The lobby of Crummer Hall displays two 1929 **Tiffany medallion windows.**

The Pursuit of Beauty

Born to the founder of one of the most prestigious jewelry companies in America, Louis Comfort Tiffany began exploring the art of glassmaking when he was 24. In 1881 Tiffany patented his opalescent window glass, which he made by combining several colors to create a wide range of different hues and three-dimensional effects. Four years later he opened his own glass-manufacturing studio. Inspired by the lush colors of flowers and plants, Tiffany worked on commission, fashioning elaborate stained-glass windows for his clients, which included many churches. In 1893 Tiffany introduced his first brilliantly colored blown-glass vases and bowls, which he called "Favrile" glass. The last house designed in its entirety by the man whose declared life's goal was "the pursuit of beauty" was his own. Tiffany completed his Laurelton Hall in Oyster Bay, Long Island, in 1904. Today the Morse Museum holds the largest collection of furniture, stained glass and architectural elements from this house.

Orange County Regional History Center ★

65 E. Central Blvd., in Heritage Sq. 407-836-8500. www.thehistorycenter.org.
Open year-round Mon–Sat 10am–5pm, Sun noon–5pm. Closed major holidays. $7.

How much do you know about Florida? See how many of the 150 moving model Florida icons you can identify—they're above your head in the two-story-tall orange dome that fills the entrance hall. Discover central Florida's colorful history in this former county courthouse (1927). Four floors of engaging exhibits, many of them interactive, tell the story of the area's past from its ancient peoples to the arrival of Disney.

Take time to watch the introductory video in a comfy rocking chair in the Orientation Theater. Then enter a re-created Timucuan village, settle into a Florida cowboy's saddle, walk within a mock citrus grove, and see how Disney's Cinderella Castle was built. On the third floor, one of the original courtrooms is open for viewing.

Orlando Museum of Art ★

2416 N. Mills Ave., in Loch Haven Park. 407-896-4231. www.omart.org. Open year-round Tue–Fri 10am–4pm, weekends noon–4pm. Closed Mon & major holidays. $6.

Rated by *Newsweek* magazine as one of the best art museums in the South, the Orlando Museum of Art began as a local art center in 1924. As the community grew, so did the museum, which doubled its gallery space in 1997. The heart of the permanent collection is rotated in four contemporary galleries. In addition to its permanent collection, the museum hosts a regular schedule of traveling exhibits.

The Permanent Collection

American Art – More than 600 works of 19C and 20C American art include paintings by John Singer Sargent, George Inness, Georgia O'Keefe, Maurice Prendergast, Childe Hassam and Gene Davis.

Art of the Ancient Americas – Pre-Columbian cultures from North America, South America and Central America are represented by pottery, jade, stone and textile artifacts dating from 2000 BC to AD 1521.

African Art – This collection features ceremonial and everyday artifacts from numerous regions, including Yoruba beadwork, Ashante statuary and Benin metalwork.

Orlando Science Center★

777 E. Princeton St., in Loch Haven Park. 407-514-2000. www.osc.org. Open year-round Mon–Thu 9am–5pm, Fri & Sat 9am–9pm, Sun noon–5pm. Closed Thanksgiving Day & Dec 25. $10.

This impressive museum, expanded to six times its original size in 1997, intrigues children and adults alike. The center's two theaters—one for large-format films and planetarium shows, and the other for live performances and science demonstrations—are complemented by the rooftop **Crosby Observatory** *(open Fri 7pm–9pm & Sat 6pm–9pm, weather permitting; $3)*, which houses Florida's largest refractor telescope.

Level 1 – The ground floor features **NatureWorks**, with lifelike dioramas of Florida ecosystems, including cypress and mangrove swamps (with real turtles and baby alligators) and a coral reef.

Level 2 – **Science City** dominates this floor with interactive displays related to mathematics, physical sciences and engineering—among them a power station and a suspension bridge. Learn about how special effects are generated by computer for the movies in ShowBiz Science.

Level 3 – **Cosmic Tourist** instructs visitors in geology and astronomy.

Level 4 – Learn about human anatomy in **BodyZone**, and help scientists unearth and study dinosaur fossils in the new exhibit, **DinoDigs**.

Where's the Fire(house)?

Between the Science Center and the Museum of Art in Loch Haven Park stands **Fire Station #3**, Orange County's oldest standing firehouse (1927). The brick structure holds Orlando's original fleet of American LaFrance fire trucks, as well as 19C and 20C fire-fighting equipment.

Orlando's arts scene is a lively mix of ballet, opera and theater performances—not bad for a town that's also home to two Hooters and the World's Largest McDonald's.

Orlando Ballet

Bob Carr Performing Arts Centre,
401 W. Livingston St. 407-426-1739. www.orlandoballet.org.

The Orlando Ballet is Central Florida's only professional dance company. Under the artistic direction of Fernando Bujones, the company presents an exciting mix of contemporary and classic programs.

Orlando Broadway Series

Bob Carr Performing Arts Centre. 401 W. Livingston St.
407-423-9999. www.orlandocentroplex.com.

A visit to Orlando is a perfect excuse to catch a Broadway show without New York City's dicey weather and rude cabbies. Recent shows have included *Aida*, *42nd Street*, and *Seussical: The Musical*.

That's Entertainment

Consult the arts and entertainment section of the *Orlando Sentinel (Fri)*, *Travelhost* and *See Orlando* for schedules of cultural events and entertainment. For arts and sporting-events tickets, contact Ticketmaster *(407-839-3900; www.ticketmaster.com)*.

Orlando Opera Company

Bob Carr Performing Arts Centre. 401 W. Livingston St. 407-426-1700. www.orlandoopera.org.

The Orlando Opera Company has brought national and international stars to the stage, including mezzo-soprano Cecilia Bartoli.

Orlando Philharmonic Orchestra

Various locations; season runs Sept-Mar. 407-896-6700. www.orlandophil.com.

The well-regarded Orlando Philharmonic typically offers a varied repertoire. Featured concerts for the past season included "O'Connor: Master of the Strings" and "Mozart: His Final Year," featuring Courtenay Budd.

T.D. Waterhouse Centre

1 Magic Place. 407-649-2255. www.orlandocentroplex.com.

When big acts like Justin Timberlake, Christina Aguilera and Jerry Seinfeld come to town, this is where they perform. The 18,000-seat arena hosts a full spectrum of events ranging from bull riding to the latest pop princess.

Culture On The Cheap

If you're planning to take in a show, check out **Otix!** first. Half-price tickets for same-day performances are available for more than 90 cultural offerings, including Cirque du Soleil, Orlando Broadway Series and Orlando Philharmonic. You can purchase Otix! tickets at the Orlando Visitor Center *(8723 International Dr., 407-363-5872; www.orlandoinfo.com)*.

Gardens

Sunshine every day—well, almost!—and subtropical weather make this region prime growing territory for lush gardens and magnificent flowers. Here are some of Orlando's most vibrant displays.

Epcot★★★

Take I-4 West to Exit 67B; go west to Epcot Center Dr. and follow signs to park entrance on left. 407-824-4321. www.disneyworld.com. World Showcase open daily 11am (10am in summer); closing times vary. $52 (ages 10 & over), $42 (ages 3–9).

Epcot's gardens are absolutely first-rate. If you're a lover of fragrant blooms, you could easily spend days roaming the grounds, strolling the paths and smelling the flowers—some 3 million plants and 10,000 fragrant roses. Green-thumb types should consider signing on for the special behind-the-scenes **Gardens of the World Tour**. This three-hour walking tour reveals the special effects and design concepts of several World Showcase gardens. Sign up at The Land pavilion.

Epcot Goes Green
The month of May is a gardener's bonanza at Epcot. This is when the park hosts **Epcot's International Flower & Garden Festival**, a celebration of horticulture featuring millions of blossoms, topiary designs, demonstrations, workshops, guest speakers, guided tours, how-to sessions, and world-class horticulture displays.

Historic Bok Sanctuary★★

55mi south of Orlando. Take I-4 West to US-27 South. Take US-27 South 23mi to Burns Ave. (Rte. 17A) and follow signs to the gardens at 1151 Tower Blvd. 863-676-1408.

www.boktower.org. Open year-round daily 8am–6pm. $8.

Ever-changing splashes of color are painted seasonally on this green canvas of meandering paths set amid lush stands of live oaks, conifers, palm trees and ferns. Begin at the **visitor center** *(follow signs from parking area)* to view an introductory film and see displays on the gardens' history. From here, wander along the bark-mulched paths, where azaleas *(Dec–Mar)* and camellias *(Nov–Mar)* color the landscape. **Window by the Pond**, a small wooden hut fitted with a large plate-glass window, welcomes visitors to sit and watch the play of life unfolding in a freshwater pond. The marble **excedra,** a monumental semi-circular conversation seat, marks the 298ft summit of Iron Mountain, considered the highest point in Florida.

Tower – Encircled by a placid moat, the 205ft tower *(interior not open to the public)* of pink-and-gray-streaked Georgian marble and buff-colored coquina is the focal point of the gardens. The Gothic Revival shaft is decorated with turquoise and brown earthenware tiles, carved sculptures and friezes, and intricately wrought ironwork. Designed in England, its **carillon** of 60 chromatically pitched bronze bells is operated by hammers from a keyboard located on the sixth level.

Harry P. Leu Gardens★

1920 N. Forest Ave. Purchase tickets in the Garden House. 407-246-2620. www.leugardens.org. Open year-round daily 9am–5pm. Closed Dec 25. $4.

If you live in a climate where nothing flowers in winter, you'll drool over the 2,000-plus **camellia collection** at Leu Gardens, in peak bloom from December to mid-February. Orlando businessman and exotic-plant collector Harry P. Leu donated his house and 50-acre botanical reserve to the city in 1961. Situated along the southern shore of Lake Rowena, the gardens also contain the largest formal **rose garden** in the state *(in bloom Mar–Jan)*, consisting of 1,000 roses representing 250 varieties. Built as a farmhouse in 1888, the two-story white frame **Leu House Museum** was enlarged by subsequent owners—including the Leu family, who lived here from 1936 to 1961 *(visit by guided tour only; closed July)*. The **Garden House** holds a gift shop, classrooms and meeting space.

The Man Behind The Gardens

Born in the Netherlands, **Edward William Bok** (1863–1930) worked in US publishing houses before founding his own publishing company in 1886. In 1920 his autobiography, *The Americanization of Edward Bok*, won a Pulitzer Prize. Bok decided to create a nature sanctuary as a gift to the American people. He invited Frederick Law Olmsted Jr., son of the famed creator of New York City's Central Park, to transform a sandy, pine-covered site atop Iron Mountain into a botanical haven. The 130-acre park was dedicated in 1929 at ceremonies led by President Calvin Coolidge.

Much the way Las Vegas seems to spring out of the surrounding desert, Orlando has erupted out of the orange groves and sleepy suburbs that encircle it, a colorful jumble of commerce amidst the central Florida flatlands. Although the commercial stuff has, inevitably, spread to nearby towns, there's still a good bit of undeveloped countryside left intact. A short drive will get you to fragrant piney woodlands, pristine hardwood hammocks, and dazzling beaches dotted with bird life. You'll find numerous opportunities to glimpse Florida wildlife, perhaps even get into the water with the state's most beloved creature, the West Indian manatee. Imagine how nice it will be to show the kids wildlife that's actually *real!*

Merritt Island National Wildlife Refuge★★

45mi east of Orlando. Take Rte. 50 East to US-1; turn left and continue to Titusville. The refuge is 4mi east of Titusville on Rte. 402. 321-861-0667. www.merrittisland.fws.gov. Open year-round daily dawn–dusk. Closed 24hrs prior to shuttle launches.

More than 500 types of animals, including some endangered and threatened species such as the southern bald eagle, the manatee and the loggerhead sea turtle, find refuge on these 14,000 acres owned by NASA. Besides offering terrific wildlife-watching opportunities, the refuge provides a peek at how the Florida coast looked before humans intruded. About 1,500 acres of parkland are devoted to citrus groves, some of which existed before NASA bought the land in the early 1960s.

The **visitor center** on Route 402 has information on wildlife in the surrounding marshes, hardwood hammocks and pine flatwoods. **Playalinda Beach★★** *(6mi east of the visitor center)* offers 4mi of beautiful, unspoiled beach, without a high rise in sight—OK, except for the Vehicle Assembly Building and the two shuttle launchpads on the southern horizon. Advanced technology seems incidental here, where pelicans skim the surf and sea oats bend in gentle breezes. The beach is part of **Canaveral National Seashore**, which extends 22mi north to Apollo Beach *(clothing is optional at the north end of Playalinda Beach).*

Black Point Wildlife Drive★ – Don't miss this 7mi, self-guided driving tour along a one-lane dirt road that crosses a dike built in the 1950s to control mosquitoes. A short trail leads to an observation tower, plus, several turnouts offer opportunities to view shorebirds.

Ocala National Forest ★★

90mi north of Orlando. From Ocala, take Rte. 40 East 11mi to the forest visitor center. 10863 E. Rte. 40. 352-236-0288. www.southernregion.fs.fed.us/florida. Open year-round daily 8am–8pm. Closed Dec 25. $2–$4 (depending on area).

When they say "Big Scrub" here they're not talking about cleaning the kitchen. They're talking about Ocala National Forest, known locally as "Big Scrub" for its predominance of scrub sand pine and oaks. Established in 1908, Ocala National Forest is the oldest national forest east of the Mississippi. Encompassing some 383,000 acres of wetlands, timber and scrub, dotted with freshwater lakes and springs, the forest stretches about 60mi from southern Marion County up to Lake Ocklawaha. To the west lies the Ocklawaha River; the St. Johns River and Lake George mark the eastern boundary. A haven for hikers of all abilities, the park offers trails of varying length *(.5mi to 7mi)* through diverse habitats. A 67mi stretch of the **Florida National Scenic Trail** also threads through the forest. The north-south route, marked by orange blazes, winds through scrub pine, live oak and juniper stands and skirts lakes and springs.

Springs Have Sprung

Visitors to Ocala National Forest are in for a treat—some of Central Florida's most beautiful natural springs grace this vast wilderness. Picturesque **Juniper Springs** *(17mi east of the visitor center on Rte. 40; 352-625-2808)* features a palm-fringed swimming area, and a short nature trail through subtropical foliage and past bubbling spring "boils." The 7mi trip down Juniper Creek through the Juniper Prairie Wilderness is a popular canoe run. Clear waters draw snorkelers, boaters and scuba divers to **Alexander Springs** *(10mi southeast of Juniper Springs on Rte. 445).* The combination of freshwater and saltwater flowing into the headspring at **Salt Springs** *(junction of Rtes. 19 & 314; boat and canoe rentals, 352-685-2255)* creates differences in salinity at different depths, causing objects viewed underwater to appear unusually distorted. Popular with snorkelers, **Silver Glen Springs** is surrounded by ancient Indian shell mounds *(8mi north of the junction of Rtes. 19 & 40).*

Crystal River ★

86mi west of Orlando. Take Rte. 50 West to the Florida Tpk. Take the turnpike northwest to the junction with I-75 and follow I-75 North to Exit 329; follow Rte. 44 to Crystal River. Tourist information: Citrus County Chamber of Commerce, 28 NW Hwy. 19; 352-795-3149 or www.citruscountychamber.com.

Of the 30 natural springs that feed Crystal River, 28 form headwaters at **Kings Bay**, the only area in Florida where people may swim and interact directly with manatees. Considered one of the state's most important **manatee sanctuaries**, the bay harbors some 200 of the gentle sea cows each winter.

Numerous local outfitters offer dive and snorkeling trips, boat and scuba rentals, and guided boat tours of the river and bay *(check with local dive operators, or at the refuge office: 352-563-2088).* The best time to see manatees is January through March. Recreational water-use regulations—including strict boat speed limits—are enforced to protect the manatees.

Crystal River National Wildlife Refuge – Kings Bay also forms the focal point of this refuge, which encompasses nine small, undeveloped bay islands accessible only by boat *(352-563-2088; www.crystalriver.fws.gov).*

Silver Springs★

86mi north of Orlando. Take the Florida Tpk. northwest to the junction of I-75 and follow I-75 North to Exit 352. Continue on Rte. 40 East (Silver Springs Blvd.) through Ocala to Silver Springs. 352-236-2121. www.silversprings.com. Open year-round daily 10am–5pm. $32.99.

Even Disney couldn't have imagined such a splendid natural setting—a sub-tropical hammock surrounding 50 natural springs at the head of the Silver River sets the scene for this 350-acre nature park. Together the waters form the largest artesian spring in the world, producing about 5,000 gallons per second (which would fill an Olympic-size swimming pool in two minutes). Timucuan Indians worshiped the sparkling waters as the "shrine of the water gods." Visitors here began arriving by steamboat as early as the 1860s—making Silver Springs the oldest attraction in Florida.

Irresistibly touristy **glass-bottom boat rides** provide a clear view of the under-water world of the main spring, including several caverns (the deepest is 81ft) that contain fossilized bones of Pleistocene animals. Waters here are so pure (98 percent) that they have been the setting for *Tarzan* movies and the James Bond film *Moonraker*.

Big Gator Lagoon — You'll see three dozen big gators in this natural cypress swamp from the safety of elevated boardwalks.

Doolittle's Petting Zoo — Next to Jeep Safari visitors can feed giraffes, llamas, pygmy goats and baby deer.

Florida Natives Exhibit — Showcases the Sunshine State's native critters—including snakes, tortoises, spiders and mammals. Be sure to see the three animal shows offered several times a day.

Jungle Cruise — From Ross Allen Island, catch this cruise down the Fort King Waterway past an open-air zoo of exotic animals.

Lost River Voyage — This one stops at an animal rehabilitation post.

Jeep Safari — Travels through a natural habitat, where birds and animals fly and roam freely. Residents include vultures, egrets, armadillos, rhesus monkeys and Amazonian two-toed sloths (which eat, sleep, mate and give birth while upside down).

Ocala★

75mi north of Orlando. Follow the Florida Turnpike north to I-75 North, to Exit 352. Tourist Information: 352-629-8051 or www.ocalacc.com.

Horsy and hilly, Ocala's countryside ambience seems a world apart from Orlando. The "Lexington of the South," as it has been dubbed, Ocala is home to some 400 farms for Arabians, Clydesdales, thoroughbreds and quarter horses. The area is known for training and breeding, and has produced numerous North American champions and several Kentucky Derby winners. For a view of area farms, resplendent in rolling pasture and magnificent live oaks, drive south of the city on SW 27th Avenue (Rte. 475A) or SE 3rd Avenue (Rte. 475).

Homosassa Springs Wildlife State Park

89mi northwest of Orlando. 7mi south of Crystal River. 4150 S. Suncoast Blvd. 352-628-5343. www.dep.state.fl.us/parks. Open year-round daily 8am–sunset. $3.25/car.

The main attraction here is a boat ride to see manatees and other wildlife. Homosassa Springs, the 45ft-deep natural spring forming the headwaters of the Homosassa River, provides a sanctuary for manatees. The animals here have been treated for injuries sustained in boating accidents: some are released back into the

wild; others stay at the park. An underwater observatory offers close-up looks at the manatees, as they paddle languidly through schools of speckled trout, redfish, jack crevalle and snook. (Here the visitors are behind glass, not the manatees.) The 185-acre park is also a refuge for injured and orphaned bobcats, Florida black bear, the endangered American crocodile, alligators, river otters and birds of prey. Manatee programs and wildlife encounters are offered several times each day.

Florida's Gentle Giant

With its sausage-shaped body, gentle nature and doleful expression, the **West Indian manatee** is one of the most beloved members of Florida's varied and extensive family of wildlife. This curious creature is a marine mammal, but is unrelated to the whale, seal or dolphin. Its closest relative is, in fact, the elephant, although the manatee's two front flippers contain the same bones (arranged differently) as the human hand.

The herbivorous manatee has earned the nickname "sea cow," for its habit of grazing on aquatic vegetation—consuming as much as 100 pounds per day. On such a diet, an adult manatee can measure up to 13ft long and weigh as much as 3,000 pounds. Manatees frequent rivers, estuaries, bays and canals. While these animals once flourished, it is estimated that only some 3,000 of them survive in Florida. All now reside in the southeast, traveling to the Carolinas and Louisiana in the summer, and spending the winter in Florida's warm, spring-fed rivers, which maintain a constant temperature of 72–74°F. (Manatees cannot survive for extended periods in water colder than 68°F).

Manatees have no natural enemies, but development of the state's coastal areas has diminished feeding grounds, forcing the slow-moving mammals into boating areas where they often become tangled in fishing lines and injured or killed in collisions. Boat strikes currently rank as the leading human-related cause of manatee mortality in Florida.

In 1973 manatees were listed as endangered species; to further protect them, the entire State of Florida was established as a manatee sanctuary in 1978. To adopt a manatee, contact **Save the Manatee Club** *(800-432-5646)*. Funds go toward education, research and lobbying efforts.

One can only take so much Mickey. Besides, if you've come all the way to Orlando, you owe it to yourself to sample the pure pleasures of the place, the only-in-Orlando attractions that local folks have come to love. So, in the spirit of adventure and discovery, here are the "musts" for the classic Orlando experience.

Gatorland★

6mi north of Kissimmee at 14501 S. Orange Blossom Trail (US-17/92/441). 407-855-5496 or 800-393-5297. www.gatorland.com. Open year-round daily 9am–dusk. $19.95 adults, $9.95 children.

What this animal park lacks in high-tech gloss, it makes up for with a rustic charm reminiscent of 1950s-era roadside attractions. Gatorland, in fact, was founded in 1949 as an amusement park/alligator farm, selling the reptiles for their meat and skins. The 110-acre property still serves as a commercial alligator farm. Gatorland residents have been featured in TV commercials and in movies, including *Indiana Jones and the Temple of Doom*.

Enter Gatorland through a gaping, tooth-filled gator's jaw, and plan your visit (three hours should do it) around the live shows featuring gator wrestling, snakes of Florida, and the Gator Jumparoo show. Beyond its hokier charms, the park, set amidst a cypress swamp, reveals a nice slice of Old Florida. You'll develop a healthy respect for the alligators and all of the creatures here (which makes it that much harder when you notice the gator chowder on the restaurant menu, and the alligator belts they sell in the gift shop).

Gator Jumparoo – This highlight features alligators that lunge 4ft out of the water to be hand-fed a snack of chicken parts. (Now *that's* entertainment!) The gator wranglers and snake handlers share information about their charges in a folksy way, peppered with advice like, "Never insult an alligator until you've crossed the river."

Observation Tower – Enjoy views of the park and its 10-acre wading-bird sanctuary and rookery. From February through the summer, look for snowy egrets, herons and other shorebirds, who build their nests along the alligators' breeding marsh.

Disney Character Meal

At various Walt Disney World resort hotels and all Disney theme parks. Park admission is required for theme-park character dining. Reservations can be made up to 60 days in advance. 407-939-3463. www.disneyworld.com.

OK, we promised no Mickey in this section—but a Disney Character Dining Experience is definitely a must-do for families with small children. While actually meeting your favorite Disney character is a bit of a crapshoot when you're doing the park—lines get long, kids get suddenly shy when faced with a larger-than-life Pluto—the character meal is a sure-fire way to get some face-time with the characters.

Each meal features a selection of characters, and *every character stops at each table*—they promise. Meals are generally buffet-style and offer the usual assortment of fare for kids. While you're required to pay park admission to eat at theme-park restaurants, you need not be a Disney resort guest to partake in a character meal at a resort. Meal prices are about the same wherever you go, so pick a place you're dying to see (perhaps the inside of Cinderella Castle, or Disney's Polynesian Resort). Then be sure to find out which of Disney's A-list characters will show up for the meal (heaven forbid the little darlings see Pooh and Piglet if their hearts were set on Minnie and Mickey!).

Eating Along I-Drive

If you skipped dinner at Lulu's, not to worry—there are 150, yes, 150—restaurants along I Drive, and most of them have a theme so they'll stand out from the crowd. Who can resist **Race Rock Orlando,** a restaurant owned by a group of racing legends, decked out with racecars, race boats, and *Bigfoot,* the world's largest monster truck? Although that would mean passing up **Bergamo's,** where singing waiters croon show tunes, Italian ballads and opera.

Table-hopping With Mickey

Although the line-up may change, here's a quick rundown of who's currently appearing on the Disney celebrity dining circuit.

In the Magic Kingdom, Cinderella and friends dine at **Cinderella's Royal Table** at Cinderella Castle *(breakfast)*; Winnie the Pooh and chums show up for all three meals at the **Crystal Palace**; while Minnie, Pluto and Goofy dine nightly at **Liberty Tree Tavern** *(from 4pm)*. At Epcot, join Mickey and friends for all three meals at **Garden Grill Restaurant** in The Land. At Disney-MGM Studios, Minnie, Goofy, Pluto and Chip 'n' Dale make the scene at **Hollywood & Vine** *(breakfast & lunch)*. At Disney's Animal Kingdom, the A-list (Mickey, Goofy, Donald, Pluto) turns up at Donald's Breakfastosaurus buffet at **Restaurantosaurus** in Dinoland U.S.A.

Among the Disney World resorts that host character meals are **Disney's Beach Club Resort**, **Contemporary Resort**, **Grand Floridian Resort & Spa**, **Polynesian Resort** and **Key West Vacation Club**. The folks at the main Disney Dining switchboard *(407-939-3463)* can provide details and book reservations.

Musts For Fun

International Drive

To order an International Drive Resort Area Official Visitors Guide and I-Ride Trolley Route map, call 866-243-7483 or visit www.internationaldriveorlando.com.

It's garish, it's gaudy, it's totally commercial—and those are just a few of the things you'll love about it. Far from being just another street, Orlando's International Drive has become a zone all its own—a snapshot of the city in miniature. For any visitor, an I-Drive road trip is a must-do, but don't feel you need to drive it. The best way to do International Drive is to hop on the **I-Ride trolley**—for a mere 75 cents *(one way)* you can cruise the entire 'hood, from 7am until midnight. There are 79 stops along the way on the trolley's main line alone. Be spontaneous and stop when the mood hits (i.e., "Look, honey—there's Skull Kingdom! Let's go!").

As for shopping, if you've ever dreamed it up, it's probably here—I Drive is especially big on T-shirts and souvenirs, at far lower prices than you'll pay at the theme parks. If it's serious discount shopping you seek, take the I-Ride all the way to the south end; last stop, **Orlando Premium Outlets** *(see Must Shop)*. Now, if you can only remember the way back to your hotel . . . .

Pointe*Orlando – *9101 International Dr. 407-248-2838. www.pointeorlandofl.com. Open year-round Mon–Sat 10am–10pm, Sun 11am–9pm. Many bars & restaurants stay open later.*

At this 450,00sq ft shopping/entertainment complex, you'll find 60 stores, including a huge F.A.O. Schwarz store (a 32ft Raggedy Ann marks the spot); an assortment of eateries, like **Lulu's Bait Shack** (go for a mess o' spicy shrimp); plus a 21-screen movie theater and a slew of clubs at **XS Orlando**. Housed in an upside-down building, Wonderworks *(see Musts for Kids)* keeps young ones busy with interactive science.

Skull Kingdom – *International Dr. at University Blvd. (entrance on American Way). 407-354-1564. www.skullkingdom.com. Shows year-round Mon–Fri 6pm–11pm, weekends 12pm–12am. $14.95.*

An I-Drive highlight, Skull Kingdom is two stories of haunted fun behind a gigantic skull. In this intense creep-fest, live performers, robotics and special effects try to scare the living daylights out of you.

Titanic–Ship of Dreams – *At The Mercado, 8445 International Dr. 407-248-1160. www.titanicshipofdreams. com. Open daily 10am–8pm. $16.95.*

At the world's first permanent museum devoted exclusively to the Titanic, you can see real Titanic artifacts and memorabilia from the movie, and stand on the world's first full-scale re-creation of the ship's Grand Staircase. Feeling flush? Splurge on a Titanic-logoed bathrobe, or that fabulous jeweled pendant.

Winter Park Scenic Boat Tour

312 E. Morse Blvd. 407-644-4056. www.ci.winter-park.fl.us. Another pleasant pastime, if you're in the mood for serenity, is a scenic boat tour in nearby Winter Park. This narrated, hour-long boat ride cruises along the city's lovely chain of lakes and canals, taking in lakeside mansions, Rollins College, Kraft Azalea Gardens and cypress swamps.

Lake Eola Park

Central Blvd. & Rosalind Ave., downtown Orlando. 407-246-2827. Open year-round daily 6am–midnight.

If you're suffering from theme-park over-load—too much noise, too many pyrotechnics, too much sizzling concrete—a visit to Lake Eola is the perfect antidote. With the city's skyline serving as its backdrop, the park features

a cascading fountain in the middle of the lake, picnic fields and flower-lined brick pathways for strolling. Rent one of the whimsical **swan boats** *(407-839-8899)*—who could resist?—and take a leisurely paddle around the lake. Lakeside entertainment includes FunnyEola, a free city-sponsored professional **comedy and concert series** held at the amphitheater on the second Tuesday of every month.

Lakeridge Winery & Vineyard

About 20mi west of Orlando, in Clermont. Take the East-West Expressway west to the Florida Turnpike; head north on turnpike to Exit 285 (Rte. 50 West). Follow Rte. 50 West to US-27 and go north 5.5mi to vineyard. 904-394-8627 or 800-768-WINE. www.lakeridgewinery.com. Open year-round Mon–Sat 10am–5pm, Sun 11am–5pm.

What—you've never sampled a good Florida wine? Well, here's your chance. Established in 1989, this family-run operation—Florida's largest premium winery—produces 12 different products. Under the Lakeridge and Lakeridge Reserve labels, their products have won more than 300 awards for excellence in winemaking. The Blanc Du Bois has won double gold medals in international competition. Nearly 100 acres of native muscadine and Florida hybrid bunch grapes grow in the well-drained soil, where European varieties cannot survive. A guided tour includes a 14-minute introductory video, a look at the production facility and a view of the winery and bottling room from a second-story deck. At the end of the tour, visitors head to the tasting counter to sample a spectrum of reds, whites, sparklers and blush wines. Bunch grapes are harvested in late June to early July, while muscadine grapes are picked from August to early September.

Orlando Magic

T.D. Waterhouse Center, 1 Magic Place. 407-896-2442. www.orlandomagic.com. Order tickets by phone (407-89-MAGIC or 800-4NBA-TIX) or online. Dates and ticket prices vary.

Do you believe in magic? In Orlando, *everyone's* a Magic fanatic. The NBA's Orlando Magic made it to the playoffs in the 2001, 2002 and 2003 seasons, and the team's determination earned them the respect of their fans (and, grudgingly, the competition). They finished the 2003 regular season with an above .500 record (42–40) for the 11th straight time. On the team's Web site, you can select your seats using Seats-3D, a three-dimensional tool for viewing and selecting seats. The season tips off in November at the T.D. Waterhouse Center.

Richard Petty Driving Experience

At the Walt Disney World Speedway, Magic Kingdom. 407-939-0130 or 800-237-3889. www.1800bepetty.com. Open year-round daily 8am–4pm. Closed Oct 23–26, Thanksgiving Day & Dec 25. Ride-alongs start at $89.

If rides like the Incredible Hulk don't set your heart a-thumping, maybe this will do the trick. Feel what it's like to climb behind the wheel of a 630-horsepower Winston Cup-style race car and scream down the backstretch at speeds of up to 145mph around the Walt Disney World Speedway. Or, choose to ride shotgun. With four experiences to choose from, racing enthusiasts and thrill seekers are guaranteed a memorable adventure.

With an average temperature of about 72°F, Orlando offers an awesome climate for playing outside. Even in the thick of summer (thick with humidity, that is), frequent afternoon thunderstorms tend to cool things off. Add 300 lakes to the mix, some of the best bass fishing in the state, and more than 150 golf courses within a 45-minute drive, and the lure to get outdoors is especially enticing.

Wekiwa Springs State Park

15mi north of Orlando, in Apopka. Take I-4 North to Exit 94; stay on Rte. 434 West to Wekiwa Springs Rd. and follow signs to park. 407-884-2008. www.dep.state.fl.us/parks/ district3/wekiwaspring. Open year-round daily 8am–dusk. $3.25/car.

Take a walk—or a paddle—on the wild side at this 8,000-acre state park. Located about a half-hour north of Orlando, this wilderness area appears much as it did when the Timucuan Indians lived along the river banks (they left a number of shell mounds that are still visible today). The Wekiva River, accessible here, offers wonderful canoeing—in fact, the Wekiva River/ Rock Springs Run was rated one of Florida's top canoe trails by *Paddler* magazine. The upper portion of the Wekiva is an aquatic preserve, and its entire 16mi is a **Florida State Canoe Trail**. The tea-colored waters twist through pine and hardwood uplands and dense swamplands pulsing with wildlife. Rent a canoe from the park's concessionaire (they also have trail maps), and enjoy an outdoor experience that few tourists discover.

Bay Lake Bass Fishing

At Walt DisneyWorld. 407-824-2621. www.disneyworld.com.
Bass fishing at Disney World? Believe it. Back in the 1960s, the Disney folk stocked Bay Lake with 70,000 bass. The heaviest large-mouth bass caught and recorded here was 14lb, 6oz. While you probably won't set a record yourself, the odds of snagging a 6 or 7 pounder are pretty fair. No need for a license to fish Disney waters, either. They also run two-hour guided trips; call ahead for reservations.

Golf

Duffers, rejoice! With more than 150 courses, the only problem is choosing where to play. Many top area courses welcome nonmembers.

International Golf Club – *6351 International Dr. 407-239-6909. Nonmember tee-time policy varies; call for details.* Six lakes weave through wide fairways lined with ancient oaks and cypress trees.

ChampionsGate Golf Resort – *1400 Masters Blvd., in ChampionsGate. 407-787-4653. www.championsgategolf.com.* Located just 10 minutes from the Disney parks, this award-winning 36-hole course was designed by golf great Greg Norman. Whether you play the links-style International course or the American-style National course, you'll enjoy first-class amenities such as iced towel service and a GPS caddy system.

Orange Lake Country Club – *8505 Irlo Bronson Memorial Hwy. (US-192), Kissimmee. 407-239-1050.* This club boasts a 27-hole Joe Lee-designed championship course. Tee-time reservations can be made 24 or 48 hours in advance; afternoon specials run around $35, including cart and greens fee.

Information, Please

Tee Times USA, Florida's central reservation service for golf *(800-374-8633)* provides information, books tee-times and even offers advice on where to play at private, semi-private and private courses across the state.

Stop at the **Orlando Visitor Center** *(8723 International Dr., Suite 101; 363-5872; www.orlandoinfo.com)* to inquire about discounts. Disney resort guests get a discount at Walt Disney World courses, and many hotel guests get discounted rates at a number of local courses.

Disney World – Tee off on one of six championship courses *(tee times: 407-824-2270)*. The **Osprey Ridge** course, located at Bonnet Creek Golf Club *(407-824-2675)* is considered the toughest and most interesting slice of Disney linkdom. Lakes, streams, even osprey nesting platforms are part of the scene on this very manicured rolling course. The less challenging **Eagles Pines** course, also at Bonnet Creek, is lined with pine needles and sand for a beachy look. The **Palm** and **Magnolia** courses *(407-824-2288)* are beautifully landscaped, and are best for duffers who favor long, narrow and tight links.

Tennis

O-Town has more than 800 courts for visitors. Most of the larger hotels and resorts have them; many will rent equipment, arrange lessons and even set up matches for you.

Grand Cypress Racquet Club – *At the Hyatt Regency Grand Cypress Resort, 1 Grand Cypress Blvd. 407-239-1234.* This is where the A-list players head when they come to town. You'll get state-of-the-art lessons, video analysis, hard-court play, and lots of court-time instruction.

Walt Disney World – Disney courts the tennis crowd with a host of options, including the 11-court tennis center at the **Disney Wide World of Sports** complex. Plan your visit for April and take in the US Clay Court Tennis Championships.

Musts For Kids

This is one vacation you won't have to sell to the kids. Beyond the obvious lure of the theme parks, Orlando is chock-a-block with amusements. At last count, there were six water parks and a Ripley's Believe It Or Not—that pretty much says it all!

Blizzard Beach

Just west of World Dr., adjacent to Disney's All-Star Resorts. Take I-4 West to Exit 64B. Turn right on World Dr., then left on Buena Vista Dr. and follow signs. 407-824-4321. www.disneyworld.com. Open year-round daily spring & fall. Closed Fri & Sat in winter; call for hours. $31 adults (ages 10 & up), $25 children (ages 3–9).

Among water parks, this one gets high marks for creativity. As the story goes, a freak snowstorm dumped tons of white stuff on Disney World. Ski resort operators quickly moved in to create Florida's first ski resort. Alas, temperatures quickly climbed to normal levels, leaving behind slush, bobsled rides and slalom courses—and the makings of a wild and woolly water park. Dripping icicles, patches of snow and melting ice caves carry the theme to the max. There's even a ski lodge and a working chairlift. Rating raves from intrepid teens is the Summit Plummet slide, reachable by chair lift. You ride up to the "ski jump" on top of Mount Gushmore, then freefall more than 100ft into a pool at the bottom. There's also the usual mix of inner-tube rides, rafts and wave pools. Arrive early—this place gets crowded fast, and they close the gate when they reach visitor capacity.

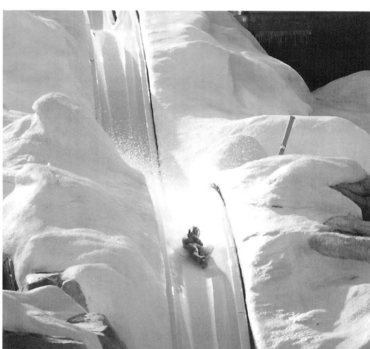

DisneyQuest

At Downtown Disney West Side. Take I-4 West to Exit 68. Turn north onto Rte. 535; turn left at first light on Buena Vista Dr.; Downtown Disney West Side extends west along Buena Vista Dr. 407-828-4600. www.disneyworld.com. Open year-round daily. Closing times vary. $31 adults (ages 10 & up), $25 children (ages 3–9).

Parents may not "get" this, but it's a sure-fire hit with kids who've moved beyond the "It's a Small World" stage. Sitting alongside other teen-oriented hangouts like House of Blues and a giant record store, DisneyQuest is a five-story "virtual adventure" entertainment center. Instead of doling out a million quarters for kids to plug into the games, you pay one fee, and then they knock themselves out in themed play areas. When hunger pangs strike, meet the kids at the Cheesecake Factory, or one of the other eateries tucked inside the Quest.

Explore Zone – Shoot prehistoric rapids, search for Incan treasure, ride Aladdin's magic carpet and fight Hades alongside Hercules.

Score Zone – Pit yourself (and your reflexes) against aliens, Mighty Ducks and comic-book super-villains.

Create Zone – A more cerebral area, where you'll learn the secrets of Disney animation and give yourself computerized makeovers.

Replay Zone – Try classic games like bumper cars—with a futuristic spin.

Tops for Thrills: Wet 'n' Wild

A more classic style of water park than Blizzard Beach, but awesome in terms of sheer adrenaline rush, is **Wet 'n' Wild** *(6200 International Dr.; 407-351-1800; wetnwild.com; open year-round daily; hours vary, check schedule online; $31.95 adults, $25.95 children (ages 3–9).* Wet 'n' Wild specializes in "wicked-steep" water slides, and activities like the Hydra Fighter—you sit in a high-powered swing and blast away with your own personal water cannon (think squirt gun on steroids). The Black Hole is a wet version of Disney's Space Mountain. Then there's Bomb Bay, where you free-fall straight down, enclosed in a capsule. This one rates high on the thrill-o-meter.

Two good reasons to opt for this park, especially if you have older kids in your party: It stays open 'til 11pm (later than Blizzard Beach) and, after 5pm, prices are slashed 50 percent. (Otherwise, rates at both places are about the same.)

Disney's Wide World of Sports

Take I-4 West to Exit 64B. Turn right on World Dr.; turn right again on Osceola Pkwy. at the first interchange, and follow signs. 407-824-4321. www.disneyworldsports.com. Open year-round daily. Hours and prices vary according to scheduled events.

This 200-acre complex has professional-caliber facilities for more than 30 competitive sports, including baseball, basketball, cycling, soccer, tennis, football, and track and field. Numerous championship, amateur and pro events happen here—plus, the Atlanta Braves of major-league baseball make Disney's 7,500-seat stadium their home for spring training. If you want to catch a game, be sure to pick up a schedule—there's something going on here every day of the year.

Ripley's Believe It Or Not Orlando Odditorium

8201 International Dr. 407-363-4418. www.ripleysorlando.com. Open year-round daily 9am–1am. $15.95 adults, $10.95 children (ages 4–12).

Ripley's is unabashedly bizarro. Even the building is weird—it's set into the ground at an angle, as though the whole thing were being sucked into a giant sinkhole. Ripley's showcases the oddities collected by Robert L. Ripley (1893–1949), an artist, explorer, collector and world-class eccentric, who devoted his life to a search for the unbelievable. Among the exhibits on display are replicas of the world's tallest man, the man with two pupils in each eye, P.T. Barnum's fake mermaid, and even an actual shrunken head. Ripley's may not be every adult's cup of tea, but the kids will get a kick out of this cheesy Orlando experience.

Wonder Works

*At Pointe*Orlando, 9101 International Dr. 407-351-8800. www.pointeorlandofl.com. Open year-round daily 9am–midnight. $16.95 adults, $12.95 children (ages 4–12).*

This interactive amusement center is built to resemble a three-story mansion turned upside down—very cool. Inside, kids sample zany activities like sitting in an electric chair, feeling the sensation of an earthquake or hurricane, creating giant bubbles, designing a roller coaster, swimming with sharks (virtually, not actually), and, weirdest of all, sitting in front of an age-progression screen to see what they'll look like in 25 years.

Must Shop

As the fastest-growing retail market in the country, Orlando offers a truly mind-boggling assortment of shopping venues, from upscale malls to giant outlet centers (and that's not counting the gift shops you'll pass through as you exit every single theme-park ride). Yes, you can find mouse-eared *everything* and giant plush Shamus, but you can also prowl through rack upon rack of discounted designer duds at local outlet malls. If you're more into atmosphere than bargain hunting, head to Winter Park, where fashionable Park Avenue offers tree-shaded shops, quaint brick streets and outdoor cafes.

Belz Factory Outlet World

5401 W. Oak Ridge Rd. at International Dr. 407-354-0126. www.belz.com/factory.

Spread over two enclosed malls and four shopping strips, Belz Factory Outlet and its more chic sibling, **Belz Designer Outlet**, offer about 200 name-brand outlet stores. Since you buy directly from the manufacturers here, you can save up to 75 percent off retail prices on sportswear, footwear, jewelry, crystal, china, watches, cameras and children's wear. Most items are first-quality overstocks, although you may encounter some irregular pieces and odd sizes. Like mining for treasure, you need to poke around to find the good stuff—it's all spread around at this megamall. Head to Mall 1 for shoes (**Bally**, **Bruno Magli**, **Stride-Rite**), and to Mall 2 for upscale kiddie duds like **Baby Guess**, and the various annexes for **Timberland**, **Tommy Hilfiger**, and so on. At Belz Designer Outlet, look for savings of 30 to 60 percent off retail on names like **Donna Karan**, **Coach Leather Goods**, **Cole Haan** and **Fossil**. Prices aren't rock-bottom, but if you have an educated eye and stick to classic styles, you can come away with a bag full of bargains that you may actually wear once you get back home.

Universal Studios Florida has its own discount store within the park, **Second Hand Rose**. Look for discounted merchandise culled from the other shops (overstocks, past-season stuff) throughout the park.

Character Duds At A Discount

Sure, you'd love to come home with some Pooh pj's or a Tower of Terror tee-shirt for the pal who walked your dog while you were away, but that souvenir-shopping tab can add up fast. Here's a tip: For last-season's Disney clothing at cheaper-than-theme-park prices, check out **Character Warehouse** at Mall 2 at Belz Factory Outlet World. You may not mind springing for that Mickey Mouse silk-screened sweatshirt if you can get it for ten bucks (versus $30 or so in the park).

Downtown Disney Marketplace

*Take I-4 West to Exit 68. Turn north onto Rte. 535; left at first light on Hotel Plaza Blvd.
Entrance to the Marketplace is at the intersection of Hotel Plaza Blvd. & Buena Vista Dr.
407-824-4321. www.downtowndisney.com.*

Looking for a bejeweled evening bag featuring Mickey's mug in Austrian crystals? Or a delightfully rakish Mickey Mouse-monogrammed silk necktie? Pasta shaped like Minnie? More Disney merchandise than you could ever imagine lures shoppers to **World of Disney**, the largest Disney store on earth. If you're a plan-ahead type, think Halloween—this store has a slew of kiddie costumes like Snow White, Winnie the Pooh, Tinkerbell and of course Mickey and Minnie.

Other standouts among the 20 or so shops at this complex include **Once Upon a Toy**, featuring new playthings designed by Disney and Hasbro that you won't find anywhere else (think Mr. Potatohead with mouse ears) and retro favorites like Lincoln Logs and Tinkertoys. The **LEGO Imagination Center** features some truly amazing—and enormous—creations built with tiny plastic Dutch bricks. (Check out the "sea monster" in Lake Buena Vista.) They offer LEGO play stations for young children, but it's not uncommon to see big people huddled around the tables as well. Other unique shops include **Magic Masters**, where you can buy magician's tools and on-site magicians will teach you how to use them; and **Starbilias**, housing one of the largest collections of celebrity memorabilia in the world.

Meanwhile, over at Disney-MGM Studios, the coolest shop is **Sid Cahuenga's One-of-a-Kind**, with bins of old movie posters, like *The Matrix* (Spanish version) and *Chitty Chitty Bang Bang*. This shop also carries signed publicity photos from the likes of Jennifer Love-Hewitt and Britney Spears.

Theme-Park Shopping

You won't have a choice but to go through the shops at the theme parks—the rides usually deposit you in a shop on your way out of the attraction. Often, you'll be too dazed to see much of anything, but a few of the shopping venues are worth checking out, because they offer something a little different than the norm.

The **Universal Studios Store** at Universal Orlando offers a fun souvenir—an Oscar statuette key chain with your name on it (unless your name is unusual, like Keanu). They also sell realistic-looking Oscar statuettes that will impress your friends—or make great centerpieces at your Academy Awards party. **Photo Funnies,** at Universal's Islands of Adventure, offers comics-related stuff like pj's printed with the Sunday funnies. Also at Islands of Adventure, make it one-stop shopping at **Adventure Trading Company**, where they've put all the goods from every island under the same roof (huggable E.T. plush sits alongside Spider-Man backpacks).

The Mall at Millenia

Take Exit 78 off I-4 to 4200 Conroy Rd. 407-363-3555. www.mallatmillenia.com.

Consider this one the flip side of the outlet malls. Very, very posh indeed, the Mall at Millenia offers valet parking, a multilingual concierge staff and 150-plus stores such as **Chanel**, **Cartier**, **Tiffany & Co.**, **Louis Vuitton**, **Gucci**, **Lacoste** and **Lillie Rubin**. Anchor stores are **Bloomingdales**, **Neiman Marcus** and **Macy's**. Mixed among these are some hipper names that appeal to 20-somethings, like Lucky Brand Jeans, Bebe, Quicksilver and Urban Outfitters. The latter offers a fun contrast to some of the more dignified designer names at this mall, with dorm room must-haves like fake fur pillows, mirrored disco balls and Mr. "T" soap-on-a-rope. There's more good browsing at the **Museum of Modern Art** store, where you'll find everything from a Van Gogh's *Starry Night* jigsaw puzzle to an Egyptian statue priced at $2,950. Meanwhile, **Tommy Bahama** features cool souvenirs with a tropical feel, like palm-tree-shaped flip-flops and coconut-scented candles.

Orlando Premium Outlets

8200 Vineland Ave. 407-238-7787.

This outdoor, Mediterranean-themed shopping village offers 110 designer-label and name-brand outlet stores, with markdowns from 25 to 65 percent. Some of these stores are the same ones that crop up at every outlet mall—others are uncommon finds that will delight the fashion-conscious in your bunch, including high-profile names like **Versace**, **Ermenegildo Zegna**, **Burberry**, **Tod's**, **Oilily**, **Escada** and **Barney's New York**. You won't get away cheaply at some of these stores, but if you've had your eye on, say, that cute Burberry plaid tote, you might walk away with it for half of what you'd pay at full retail. You might see this season's must-have white-eyelet skirt for 50 bucks, not $165, at Barney's, but only in size 2. Some of the best bargains on basics are at the **Banana Republic Factory Store**, where throngs of shoppers snap up $9.99 tees at back-to-school time.

Park Avenue in Winter Park

7mi north of Orlando in Winter Park. Take I-4 East to Exit 87 East (Fairbanks Ave.), then go 1.5mi to Park Ave. and turn left. For information, contact the Winter Park Chamber of Commerce: 407-644-8281 or www.winterparkcc.org.

Just a few minutes north of downtown Orlando, Winter Park offers a stylish shopping district with a European feel. Park Avenue boasts wrought-iron lamp-posts, old oak trees and sidewalk cafes. Health food stores, juice bars and chocolate shops intermingle with national chain stores and individually owned boutiques. Plan to stay for lunch, and spend a few minutes admiring the Tiffany stained glass at the Charles Hosmer Morse Museum of American Art *(see Museums)*, or take a scenic boat tour to make the most of your visit *(see Musts for Outdoor Fun)*.

Some of the more unique shops include **Timothy's Gallery** *(212 Park Ave. N.)* for contemporary crafts and jewelry, and **Olive This, Relish That** *(346 Park Ave. N.)* for vintage olive oils, freshly-baked scones and other gourmet goodies. At **Douglas Cosmetics** *(200 Park Ave. N.)*, the counters are always busy with moms and daughters trying on the latest eye-shadow shades, while next door, at **Aesthetics**, they're applying spray-on tans to anyone who wants a bronze glow minus the sun.

You may feel that the best thing to do after a day of theme-park hopping and outlet shopping is to crank up the air conditioner and dive under the covers. Maybe—but then you'd be missing out on Orlando's sizzling night-life scene. The mix includes a number of one-stop entertainment complexes, like Disney's Pleasure Island and Universal's CityWalk, along with some terrific haunts on downtown's Orange Avenue, if you'd rather hang with the locals.

Downtown Orlando

Downtown Orlando offers a cluster of clubs along **Orange Avenue**★, so it's easy to bar hop with the locals. If you prefer to limit your night crawling to just one spot, you won't go wrong at **The Social** *(54 N. Orange Ave.; 407-246-1599, ext. 22; www.orlandosocial.com)*. With its diverse line-up of live music, from eclectic to alternative, funk to blues to jazz, including some top names, The Social draws a wide range of ages and styles. Plus, the martinis will knock your socks off.

Hard-core party people head to the **Club at Firestone**, a former tire store *(578 N. Orange Ave.; 407-872-0066; www.clubatfirestone.com)*, where the dancing doesn't stop 'til 3am. Dress up, arrive late, and don't count on being the first one in line at Space Mountain the next day.

Cover Charges

Orlando club owners love a promotion. Ladies' nights, happy hours, bring a friend, you name it, they'll do it to get you in the door. If things are slow, they'll offer free drafts, no cover charges and $1.50 drink specials. If you want to start early, say before 9pm, you may get in for free at some clubs. Generally, expect to pay a cover charge of around $3–$6 at most clubs once the entertainment begins. If there are big names on stage, prices soar as high as $15 to $30.

Pleasure Island

Take I-4 West to Exit 68. Turn north onto Rte. 535, and left again at the first light on Hotel Plaza Blvd. Entrance to Pleasure Island is at intersection of Hotel Plaza Blvd. & Buena Vista Dr. Closes at 2am; free until 7pm. Must be 18yrs or older unless accompanied by a parent. BET Soundstage Club and Mannequins Dance Palace require proof of age (patrons must be at least 21). 407-824-4321. www.disneyworld.com.

Disney's Pleasure Island offers eight nightclubs and a commercial theater in a warehouse-type setting. Despite the loud music, a few scantily clad dancers, and alcohol served on the streets, it's still a fairly wholesome setting. The **BET Soundstage Club** delivers R&B and hip-hop sounds, while **Mannequins Dance Palace** spins contemporary dance music (the dance floor spins, too). Disco lives on at **8Trax**, where you can boogie to the BeeGees without guilt, then switch to the breezy setting of the **Rock 'N' Roll Beach Club**, where live bands

send blazing guitar riffs into the night sky. Arguably, the best live acts show up at the **Pleasure Island Jazz Company**, which consistently brings nationally recognized artists and talented unknowns to its stage. There's also **Motion**, Pleasure Island's newest club, featuring everything from Top 40 to alternative music, and improvisational comedy at the **Comedy Warehouse**. Perhaps the oddest entry at Pleasure Island is the **Adventurer's Club**, a quirky parody of a British travelers' fraternity. You'll pay one fee to get your hand stamped, then you're free to take in as much of the action as you can handle. End your evening in true Disney style, with a mock New Year's Eve celebration—complete with noisemakers, confetti, a countdown and fireworks.

Best Bar With A View

If you'd simply like a quiet place to hold hands and down a cold cocktail, you won't do better than the **Top of the Palace**, on the 27th floor of the Wyndham Palace Resort & Spa *(1900 Buena Vista Dr.; 407-827-2727; www.wyndhamorlandohotels.com)*. **Bonus:** You'll get a great view of the Magic Kingdom and its nightly fireworks show.

Universal CityWalk

1000 Universal Studios Plaza. Follow I-4 West to Exit 74. Turn right on Hollywood Way and follow signs. 407-363-8000. www.universalorlando.com. Stores and some restaurants open until 11pm or midnight; clubs generally close at 1am or 2am.

Universal's CityWalk is a two-tiered promenade of dining and entertainment venues, linked by bridges to Universal Studios Florida and Islands of Adventure. A bit hipper than the competition, CityWalk features wildly-colored buildings, free-form sculptures and streetscapes, all wrapped around a four-acre harbor. This is a high-energy hangout, punctuated by famous names.

Jimmy Buffett's Margaritaville – You can always get a "cheeseburger in paradise" at this combination nightclub and restaurant featuring Floribbean cuisine and island music.

Latin Quarter – Serves up foods from 21 Latin nations, live Latin music and dance lessons.

Bob Marley–A Tribute to Freedom – Here they've recreated the Jamaican home and garden of the reggae messiah, with Jamaican cuisine and music nightly.

CityJazz – Boasts the Thelonious Monk Institute of Jazz and a jazz hall of fame, plus the smooth sounds of master musicians in a performance venue.

Other Options at CityWalk – **Motown Café** serves American regional cuisine and features live R&B groups; **Pat O'Brien's** has Cajun-style eats and dueling pianos. There's a 2,200-seat **Hard Rock Café** and performance venue—the world's largest Hard Rock—plus **NBA City** (play interactive games and watch great NBA moments while you dine), and even a **NASCAR Café**. Those who want to skip the meal can get into **The Groove**, a nightclub with a high-tech dance floor, or simply relax with a bucket of popcorn at the 20-screen **Cineplex Odeon Theater.**

Other Adventures in Club Land

Beyond the big, multiclub entertainment scenes are a few other nighttime haunts worthy of your consideration. **Downtown Disney**, adjacent to Pleasure Island, is the home of the top-notch **House of Blues**, one of the major live-music venues in the area. The complex includes a fine restaurant, a bar and a concert hall, where marquee names have included Eric Clapton, Steve Winwood, Fiona Apple and Aretha Franklin.

The **Atlantic Ballroom** at **Disney's Boardwalk** resort is a different scene altogether. Set on the boardwalk of a re-created 1930s seaport, the dance hall is dressed up in rich blues, reds and golds, and set off by twinkling lights. Order one of their signature martinis before hitting the parquet dance floor. The retro-swing sounds will transport you to a more gracious era.

The Scoop At A Glance

To get the scoop on local action, pick up a free copy of *Orlando Weekly*, a guide to arts and entertainment happenings. It's available at selected bars, nightclubs and restaurants. Also, consult the arts and entertainment section of the Friday *Orlando Sentinel*.

If you tend to feel like you need a vacation to *recover* from your vacation, a visit to a spa might be the perfect therapy. Many Orlando hotels offer full-service spas—all the newest properties seem to have "& Spa" attached to their names—recognizing that travelers are embracing the concept of a spa escape as a must-do element of their vacations. (You don't have to be a hotel guest to take advantage of spa services, but advance booking is required.) Even Canyon Ranch has an Orlando outpost, and Disney—not to be outdone—even offers "Minnie Pampering" for little divas-in-training! A unique aspect of the Orlando spa experience is the theme-park treatments, designed to counteract the ill effects of pounding the pavement under central Florida's brutal sun.

Canyon Ranch SpaClub

Gaylord Palms Resort, 6000 W. Osceola Pkwy., Kissimmee. 407-586-0315. www.gaylordpalms.com.

This huge resort—a magnet for conventioneers—lures spa-goers with an on-site Canyon Ranch outpost. The signature treatment here is Euphoria, a two-hour pampering session. You'll start with an aromatherapy scalp massage, and then have your head wrapped in towels dipped in sage oil. Next, the therapist will apply a botanical mask to your body and buff it off. This is followed by a delicious soak in a tub filled with essential oils and rose petals, topped off by a light massage. You're sure to slink out of the spa with a smile on your face.

Celebrity Spa

Star Island Resort and Country Club, 5000 Ave. of the Stars, Kissimmee. 407-396-8300. www.star-island.com.

Leave the rest of your bunch in line at Space Mountain and sneak off to Celebrity Spa for their three-hour Spa Relaxer treatment. This includes a half-hour facial and body treatment, shampoo and hairstyling, manicure and pedicure—guaranteed to make you feel as chipper as a Disney cast member.

Disney's Grand Floridian Spa

Grand Floridian Resort and Spa, 4401 Grand Floridian Way. 407-824-3186. www.disneyworld.com.

Why should parents have all the fun? Kids age four to twelve can get buffed and polished with a 90-minute Minnie Pampering treatment, including a facial, manicure and pedicure and, of course, a kid-size bathrobe. For moms and dads, the hottest treatment these days is the hot-stone massage for body, face and feet. Combined with Swedish massage techniques and aromatherapy oils, on-the-rocks never felt so good.

Greenhouse Spa

Portofino Bay Hotel, Universal Studios Orlando, 5601 Universal Blvd. 407-224-7117.
www.loewshotels.com.

Call it the spa version of "It's a Small World." At the Portofino Bay Hotel's luscious Greenhouse Spa, guests experience a massage with 10 different cultural touches. The spa's signature Well-Being Massage, an hour-long treatment, incorporates Swedish touch, shiatsu, Hawaiian lomi lomi, Indian ayurvedic and reiki, among other types of massage. The treatment begins with a ritual cleansing of the feet with lime oil, and ends with ringing chimes, signifying that it's time to re-enter the real world.

Wyndham Palace Resort & Spa

Walt Disney World Hotel Plaza. 800-327-3906. www.wyndham.com.

The therapists at this spa deliver an awesome Theme Park Leg-Relief Massage that stimulates the circulation in the legs with essential oils. After working the leg muscles, therapists turn their attention to weary feet, with a soothing massage that leaves aching feet feeling refreshed and baby's-bottom soft.

Among other deliciously pampering procedures, the Wyndham Palace spa offers an herbal eye-lift treatment that eliminates (at least temporarily) those tiny furrows that develop from waking up at 4am to beat the crowds at the Magic Kingdom. They even offer a Water Lily Wrap featuring aloe, Vitamin E, green tea and chamomile, to relieve discomfort caused by sunburn.

More Pampering Palaces

Here are a few more places to get wrapped, rubbed and recharged during your Orlando visit: The new **Ritz-Carlton Spa** at the Ritz-Carlton Orlando Grande Lakes resort *(407-206-2400)* is O-Town's largest, with 40 treatment rooms. Some beauty treatments will feature the healing benefits of Florida citrus fruits (oranges, lemons and grapefruits). Down Disney way, **The Spa at the Disney Institute** *(407-827-7049)* offers a Warm Seafoam Mud Wrap that features sea-salt exfoliation (rubdown), followed by an application of warm mud drawn from the depths of the ocean. As the mud bubbles, a therapist massages your head and neck. (This part is especially wonderful if you've been jerked around by one too many motion simulation rides!)

Best Excursions From Orlando

Set smack-dab in the center of the Sunshine State, Orlando makes a great base for day trips and excursions to other intriguing Florida destinations. The so-called "Space Coast," featuring Kennedy Space Center, is just 45 minutes to the east. North of the space center, St. Augustine attracts visitors to America's oldest city. An hour's drive west of Orlando, the Tampa Bay area boats the city of Tampa and its Cuban-flavored district Ybor City, as well as St. Petersburg and its white-sand beaches. North of Tampa, the town of Tarpon Springs celebrates its Greek heritage in lively annual festivals.

Kennedy Space Center★★★

From Orlando, take Rte. 528 (Beeline Expwy.), about 51mi east. Kennedy Space Center is located 6mi east of US-1 on NASA Parkway. 321-449-4444. www.kennedyspacecenter.com. Open year-round daily 9am–6pm. Closed Dec. 25 & on launch days. $33 adults, $23 children (ages 3-11).

. . . 3-2-1 blastoff! Since it opened to the public in 1996, Kennedy Space Center has rocketed into popularity as one of Florida's top attractions with more than 2 million visitors touring the facility each year. Here, the world's most sophisticated technology emerges from a Florida east coast wilderness of orange groves, tidal flats and pristine beaches. Every rocket—from the one that carried the *Explorer I* satellite in 1958 to modern space shuttles—has blasted off from Merritt Island or adjoining Cape Canaveral.

Tips For Visiting

Kennedy Space Center is busiest between June and August and on holidays. Weekends are less crowded. Two restaurants, the Lunch Pad and the Orbit Cafeteria, are located on site. A costumed Spaceman roams the complex from 10:30am–5:30pm for photo ops. Movies are shown several times a day in two IMAX theaters.

Bus Tours – Most visitors take a two- or four-hour bus tour of the facility. One of the highlights includes **Launch Complex 39**, where visitors climb a 60ft observation platform and, if they're lucky, see a rocket that is waiting to take off. There's also a short film and exhibit detailing the launch procedure (NASA's disasters are not omitted). An excellent movie about the *Apollo 11* mission and a close-up inspection of a 363ft *Saturn V* moon rocket are featured in a stop at the **Apollo/Saturn V Center**. A recent addition to the complex is the **International Space Station Center**, where visitors learn about the venture that is driving the space industry in the 21C.

What A Blast!

To obtain a schedule for **shuttle launches**, visit the Web site: *www.kennedy spacecenter.com*. Launch-viewing tickets go on sale approximately six weeks prior to launch date and may be purchased online or by phone *(321-449-4444)*. For updated launch information, call 321-867-4636 or 800-KSC-INFO *(Florida only)*. If you're unable to reserve a spot at KSC to watch a launch, make a beeline for the following alternative sites (arrive early to make sure you have an unobstructed view to the east).

• Along Canaveral National Seashore

• Along Rte. 402, north of Complex 39 in Merritt Island National Wildlife Refuge *(parts of the refuge may be closed due to launch activities)*

• Along the Indian River on US-1 in Titusville between Rte. 528 and Rte. 402 *(the city permits roadside parking up to 24hrs before launch time)*

• Jetty Park *(east end of Jetty Dr.)*

• Rent a hotel room on the beach for a great vantage point

Astronauts Memorial – Behind the theaters, the memorial is a moving tribute to astronauts who have made the ultimate sacrifice. Computers keep the black-granite monolith tilted to the sun so that the names—engraved on reflective panels—will be projected on the clouds. (Names are easiest to see in the sky at sunset; weather conditions may affect visibility.)

Space Shuttle Explorer – Just to the right of the memorial, a full-scale replica of *Explorer* reveals the relative roominess of modern space vehicles compared to the claustrophobic dimensions of pioneering spacecraft.

US Astronaut Hall of Fame – Now part of the Kennedy Space Center Visitor Complex, the Hall of Fame tells the stories of America's heroes of space flight and is home to the world's largest collection of space-travel memorabilia. In the interactive **Simulator Station,** visitors can try out realistic training simula-tors to experience a moon walk, a G-force trainer and a shuttle landing. The **Exhibit Hall** features a historic col-lection of spacecraft, including the *Mercury Sigma 7* capsule and the *Apollo 14* command module.

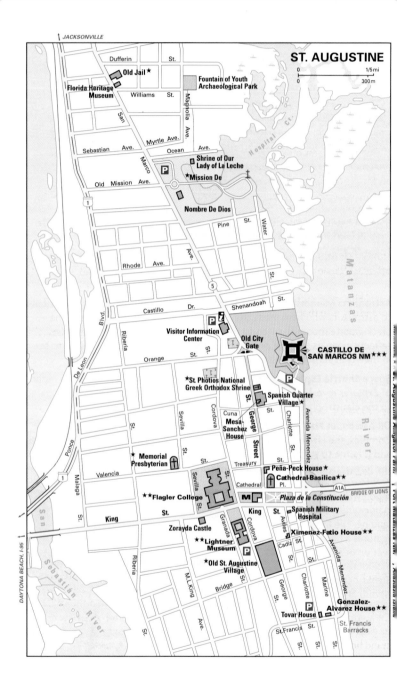

ST. AUGUSTINE

JACKSONVILLE

Dufferin St.

Old Jail ★

Florida Heritage Museum

Williams St.

Fountain of Youth Archaeological Park

Magnolia Ave.

San St.

Sebastian Ave.

Myrtle Ave.

Marco

Ocean Ave.

Old Mission Ave.

Shrine of Our Lady of La Leche

★ Mission De

Nombre De Dios

Pine St.

Water St.

Ave.

Rhode Ave.

Hospital

Matanzas

Castillo Dr.

Shenandoah St.

Riberia

Blvd.

Visitor Information Center

Old City Gate

CASTILLO DE SAN MARCOS NM ★★★

Orange St.

★ St. Photios National Greek Orthodox Shrine

Spanish Quarter Village ★

Avenida Menendez

River

De Leon

Sevilla

Cordova

Cuna St.

Mesa-Sanchez House

George Street

Charlotte St.

Ponce

★ Memorial Presbyterian

Valencia

Sevilla St.

St.

Treasury St.

Peña-Peck House ★

Cathedral-Basilica ★★

Cathedral Pl.

A1A BRIDGE OF LIONS

★★ Flagler College

Plaza de la Constitución

Malega

King St.

Zorayda Castle

King St.

Spanish Military Hospital

Granada St.

Aviles St.

Cordova St.

Ximenez-Fatio House ★★

Cadiz St.

★★ Lightner Museum

★ Old St. Augustine Village

Riberia

M.L.King Ave.

Bridge St.

George St.

Charlotte St.

Marine St.

Avenida Menendez

Gonzalez-Alvarez House ★★

Tovar House

St. Francis Barracks

St.Francis St.

San Sebastián River

DAYTONA BEACH, I-95

St. Augustine★★★

105mi north of Orlando. Take I-4 East to I-95 North to Exit 311, and follow signs into the city. Visitor center is located at 10 Castillo Dr., near San Marco Ave.; 904-829-1711; www.visitoldcity.com.

Few people boast about being old, so you might think it's strange that the city of St. Augustine advertises the fact. The oldest continuously occupied European settlement in the US—dating from 1565—St. Augustine is located on Florida's east coast on a finger of land jutting south from the mainland between two rivers (the Matanzas River on the east and the San Sebastián River on the west). Historic St. Augustine's time-burnished flavor is captured in narrow, cobbled lanes lined with buildings of pale coquina (stone formed by the sedimentation of seashells), many of them survivors of the 18C. Of course, there's a healthy sprinkling of oh-so-modern T-shirt shops and tourist attractions in the mix.

Not only is St. Augustine an easily reachable side trip from Orlando, it also offers a pleasant contrast. How refreshing to take in the oldest house/oldest jail/oldest everything after experiencing the newest/fastest/most cutting-edge! Plus, an excursion to St. Augustine provides a chance to experience something else that Orlando lacks—the ocean.

Stop at the visitor center to obtain tickets for the privately owned **sightseeing trains** that tour the city throughout the day, stopping at points of interest.

Castillo de San Marcos National Monument★★★

S. Castillo Dr. at Orange St.
904-829-6506. www.nps.gov/casa.
Open year-round daily 8:45am–4:45pm. Grounds closed midnight–5:30am. Closed Dec 25. $5.

Defender of St. Augustine since the beginning of the 18C, the oldest masonry fort in the US overlooks Matanzas Bay at the northern boundary of the old city. The Castillo withstood every enemy attack that beset it and today ranks among the best-preserved examples of Spanish Colonial fortifications in the New World.

Begin your visit by attending a ranger talk in the interior courtyard. Other rooms contain displays describing the fort's history. Don't miss the presentation of ordnance used here; from this display, you must stoop to enter a low passageway leading to the powder magazine deep in the northeast bastion. Climb the long stairway to the gundeck, outfitted with some of the castillo's original cannons and mortars. When you see the view from here, you'll understand how easy it was for sentries to monitor an enemy's approach.

The castillo served as an American military prison until the early 20C. In 1924 it was designated as a national monument.

St. George Street

After a visit to the Castillo, meander down St. George Street. The backbone of the old city retains its historic flavor despite an abundance of souvenir shops, many of which occupy restored 18C buildings. St. George Street is closed to traffic between the Old City Gate and the Plaza de la Constitución.

Cathedral-Basilica of St. Augustine★★

North side of Plaza de la Constitución. 904-824-2806. www.thefirstparish.org.

A scalloped facade and tower mark the home of the parish of St. Augustine, probably founded in 1565, and therefore ranking as the oldest Catholic parish in the nation. Inside, massive decorated timbers support the lofty ceiling above floors of colorful Cuban tile. A large, ornamental reredos of gold and white wood, incorporating the marble altar table from the original church, highlights the sanctuary.

Now That's A Fort

The increasing threat from English, Dutch and French forces convinced Spanish officials in Madrid that St. Augustine needed a permanent stone fortification. By 1695 the Castillo was largely complete. Four-sided, with pointed triangular bastions at each corner, the structure boasted 12ft-thick outer walls. Lower walls were sloped outward to counter artillery fire. As a further deterrent, a broad moat surrounded the fort.

In 1740 English warships under General James Oglethorpe bombarded the fort for 27 days. Their cannonballs sank into the soft coquina walls, however, and did little damage. The castillo was handed over to British authority in 1763, when Florida was transferred from Spain to Great Britain. Spain recovered it at the close of the Revolutionary War. In 1821 the Spanish flag was lowered here for the last time as Spain ceded Florida to the US.

Flagler College★★

74 King St. Interior accessible by guided tour only. 904-829-6481. www.flagler.edu.

Formerly the Ponce de Leon Hotel, this eye-catching pink Spanish Renaissance structure was the cornerstone of Henry Flagler's master plan to transform St. Augustine into an American resort destination. Closed in 1967, the hotel building now houses the facilities of Flagler College. It's worth taking a tour to see the interior, which was designed by glass artist Louis C. Tiffany and incorporates the original oak wainscoting, leaded-glass windows and whimsical, lion's-head light fixtures.

Lightner Museum ★★

75 King St., across from Flagler College.
904-824-2874. www.lightnermuseum.org.
Open year-round daily 9am–5pm. Closed
Dec 25. $6.

Across the street from Flagler College sits yet another spectacular example of Spanish Renaissance design, Lightner Museum—formerly Henry Flagler's Hotel Alcazar *(see p 98)*. Today the corridors and the rooms where guests once stayed contain a wild assortment of **decorative arts and collectibles**, everything from art glass and antiques to fruit-crate art and campaign buttons. The museum's namesake, Otto C. Lightner, was a Chicago publisher who, no surprise, produced a magazine focusing on collectibles.

First Floor – Sciences, natural and human, are the focus of exhibits here; weights and scales, mineral collections and drafting tools are presented as if they were in a Victorian-era exhibition hall. Don't miss the steam engine created of blown glass.

Second Floor – The hotel's main baths house Lightner's extensive collection of **art glass**. From Bohemian to Bristol, the handsomely displayed pieces include designs by Louis Comfort Tiffany.

Third Floor – Lightner's decorative-arts collection includes intricately carved 19C furniture from India, samplers stitched in the 18C, and an Art Nouveau parlor suite.

The Man With The Plan

Florida owes much of its success as tourist destination to one man: **Henry Morrison Flagler** (1830–1913). The son of an itinerant Presbyterian minister, Flagler was born in Hopewell, New York. At age 14, sick of school, he set out to Ohio to make his fortune. There he landed a job in a general store for $5 a month, and soon developed a knack for salesmanship. Eventually Henry entered into partnership with his friend, wealthy industrialist John D. Rockefeller. Their oil refinery, incorporated in 1870 as Standard Oil Co., established huge fortunes for the two influential men.

Flagler visited Florida in 1877 on the advice of doctors treating his invalid wife, Mary. Widowed by 1883, Flagler honeymooned in St. Augustine with his second wife. The businessman shrewdly observed that while its agreeable climate drew wealthy winter visitors, the city offered few amenities. Two years later, Flagler had hatched a scheme to transform St. Augustine into a resort rivaling France's Riviera. His plan involved building a hotel and linking his railway with big cities along the Eastern seaboard.

Flagler's massive Ponce de Leon Hotel, its less elegant counterpart the Hotel Alcazar, and the Casa Monica Hotel, a large property that he purchased, formed the basis of St. Augustine's heyday as Florida's premier resort destination. Flagler eventually acquired additional rail lines to found the **Florida East Coast Railway**, which he extended south from Daytona to Miami via Palm Beach . . . and, well, you know the rest of the story.

Gonzalez-Alvarez House (The Oldest House)★★

14 St. Francis St. (between Charlotte & Marine Sts.). Visit by guided tour only.
904-824-2872. www.oldcity.com/ oldhouse. Open year-round daily 9am–4:30.
Closed Easter Sunday, Thanksgiving Day & Dec 25. $6.

Here we go with the "oldest" claims again: This handsome National Historic Landmark is believed to be St. Augustine's oldest residence. Initially a flat-roofed coquina building with tabby floors, the house was built in the early 18C for Tomás Gonzalez y Hernandez, a settler from the Canary Islands. The Geronimo Alvarez family purchased the house in 1790 and it passed through several generations of that family before being sold in 1882.

With its rugged tabby floors and exposed coquina walls, the gloomy lower level reveals the spartan lifestyle of the Gonzalez family, while the upstairs reveals the relative comfort enjoyed by the Alvarez family.

The Hotel Alcazar: Then and Now

Henry Flagler commissioned this hotel as a less luxurious alternative to the Ponce de Leon Hotel. Designed by noted architects Carrère and Hastings, the poured-concrete structure boasted shops and a casino annex with a large swimming pool, ballroom, bowling alley, billiards room and a gymnasium.

To Flagler's surprise, guests preferred the relaxed atmosphere of the Alcazar to its more formal sister, and the hotel soon outstripped the Ponce de Leon in popularity. The same economic factors that slowed business at the Ponce also proved the Alcazar's undoing. The hotel closed its doors for good in 1937.

In 1946, empty and forlorn, the building was purchased by Chicago publisher Otto C. Lightner. By 1947 Lightner had installed his vast assemblage of stuff in the corridors of Hotel Alcazar; today his collection occupies the former spa and gymnasium. The casino and ballroom have been restored, and an antiques mall and cafe occupy the pool basin.

St. Augustine Alligator Farm★★

999 Anastasia Blvd. (South Rte. A1A), 1mi south of the Bridge of Lions. 904-824-3337 or 877-966-7275. www.alligatorfarm.com. Open year-round daily 9am–5pm (until 6pm in summer). $14.95.

Have you come all the way to Florida and not seen an alligator yet? Well, about 2,500 crocodilians live here, in landscaped habitats and re-created swamps. Plan to attend the informative shows in the reptile theater, where knowledgeable staff handle Florida snakes and even a white alligator. You may wonder if the alligators sunning themselves in the main pen are alive, since they stay immobile for long periods (they are). Don't miss the **Land of Crocodiles**, Alligator Farm's outstanding—and rare—collection of all 22 species of crocodilians. The **wading-bird rookery** is home to egrets, herons and wood storks during the nesting season.

> ### Gomek: Gone, But Not Forgotten
>
> A special indoor exhibit at St. Augustine Alligator Farm, called Gomek Forever, honors a 1,700-pound saltwater crocodile from New Guinea who was the park's star resident from 1990 until his death in 1997. Now mounted, Gomek consumed 100 pounds of nutria and chicken a week during the warm season while he was alive (most crocodilians don't eat in cold weather).

Ximenez-Fatio House★★

20 Aviles St. Visit by guided tour only. 904-829-3575. www.ximenezfatiohouse.org. Open year-round Mon–Sat 11am–4pm. Closed Sun. $5.

For a look at the way early St. Augustine buildings were adapted for various uses, tour this two-story coquina residence. Operated as a boardinghouse for most of the 19C, the structure was built in 1798 by Spanish merchant Andrés Ximenez as his residence and general store. Under a later owner, the establishment thrived as St. Augustine's most popular inn. Today the house is restored to reflect the period between 1830 and 1850; individual rooms are furnished as if to accommodate 19C boarders.

Government House Museum★

[M] refers to map p 94. 48 King St. 904-825-1000. www.historicstaugustine.com. Open year-round daily 9am–5:30pm. Closed Dec 25. $2.50.

The stately, two-story masonry Government House served St. Augustine's officials for nearly 400 years. First constructed in 1599, the house ultimately became the official governor's residence. A crumbling hulk by 1687, it was rebuilt of more durable coquina, but succumbed to fire during the British attack in 1702. After 1821 the US government used the rebuilt structure as a courthouse. Today Government House serves as a museum and headquarters of the Historic St. Augustine Preservation Board.

Inside, the small museum provides a look at the development of St. Augustine through colorful displays that illustrate the cultural collage of settlers who lived here over the years.

Mission de Nombre de Dios★

San Marco Ave. & Ocean Ave. 904-824-2809. Open year-round daily 8am–5:30pm, weekends 9am–5pm. Closed major holidays.

A 208ft stainless-steel cross marks the approximate spot where Pedro Menéndez de Avilés and his men came ashore to take possession of Florida for Philip II of Spain in 1565. Menéndez' chaplain marked the event by celebrating Mass, thus establishing the Mission de Nombre de Dios, the first Catholic mission in the US. Though nothing remains today of the original structures, the gleaming cross, erected in 1966 to commemorate the 400th anniversary of the founding of St. Augustine, still looms above the salt marsh. Paths lead to an ivy-covered chapel housing the Shrine of Our Lady of La Leche, originally erected here in 1613 by Spanish settlers.

Old St. Augustine Village★

250 St. George St. (entrance on Bridge St.). 904-823-9722. www.old-staug-village.com. Open year-round daily 9am–5pm. Closed Thanksgiving Day & Dec 24–25. $5.

Nine historic houses (five of which are open to the public), dating from 1790 to 1910, occupy a full city block *(bounded by St. George, Bridge and Cordova Sts. & St. Joseph Convent)* that formed part of the original 16C walled colonial town. The oldest is the Prince Murat House (1790), once home to Achille Murat, nephew of Napoleon Bonaparte. A Spanish Colonial constructed of coquina, the house contains Murat's father's bed from Château de Versailles outside Paris. Throughout the village, interpreters provide entertainment.

Spanish Quarter Village★

53 St. George St. 904-825-6830. Open year-round daily 9am–5:30pm. Closed Thanksgiving, Dec 25 & Jan 1. $6.50.

Eight buildings at this living-history museum re-create the later years of the city's first Spanish period. Enter through Florencia House and walk the grassy "streets" of St. Augustine, c.1740. The dwellings of a foot soldier, an artillery sergeant and a cavalryman reveal the variations in wealth, rank and status of soldiers based at the Castillo. A smithy works in the restored blacksmith shop, while costumed interpreters demonstrate everyday activities from the 18C.

Marineland ★

18mi south of St. Augustine via A1A at 9600 Ocean Shore Blvd. 904-460-1275 or 888-279-9194. www.marineland.net. Open year-round daily 9: 30am–4:30pm. Closed Dec 25. Check schedules at entrance for times of shows and oceanarium feedings. $14.

This Old Florida oceanfront park, straddling A1A, was conceived as an underwater film studio. Founders included Cornelius Vanderbilt Whitney, great-grandson of transportation magnate Cornelius Vanderbilt, and Ilia Tolstoy, grandson of renowned Russian author Leo Tolstoy. Opened in 1938 to shoot footage of marine life, the studio quickly became a tourist attraction. Techniques for photographing dolphin behavior and recording dolphin sounds were pioneered here.

Dolphins swim right up to visitors at the **Top Deck** of the circular oceanarium, also the site of dolphin shows. Dolphins-in-training perform throughout the day at the **Dolphin Stadium**. Crowd-pleaser C.J. the sea lion shows off classic tricks, like catching a ball on his nose, at the **Sea Lion Showcase**.

Fountain Of Youth

Most people immediately think of Ponce de Leon's fabled fountain of youth when they think of St. Augustine. Sad to say, neither the Spanish explorer nor modern cosmetics companies have discovered the secret of eternal youth. Even so, the **Fountain of Youth Archaeological Park** *(11 Magnolia Ave.; 904-829-3168; www.fountainofyouth florida.com; open year round daily 9am–5pm; $6)* is definitely worth a visit—even if a drink of sulphurous water from the small spring at this privately owned park does nothing more than quench your thirst!

Staying in St. Augustine

Casa Monica Hotel *–95 Cordova St. 904-827-1888 or 800-648-1888. www.casamonica.com. 138 rooms.* **$$$** Downtown's resurrected Medieval-style fort was built in 1888 as a winter getaway for America's wealthiest families. Its regal features—towers and hand-painted tiles, iron four-poster beds—will make you think you've landed in Moorish Spain. Decorated with velvets and tapestry fabrics in jewel tones, accommodations boast amenities fit for modern-day royalty.

St. Francis Inn *– 279 Saint George St. 904-824-6068 or 800-824-6062. www.stfrancisinn.com. 17 rooms.* **$$$** In America's ancient city, no place radiates more warmth than this 1791 vine-covered inn on a cobblestone lane. A fountain bubbles in the brick patio; the placid pool beckons swimmers just beyond. Plush quilts, fringed lamps and vintage photos adorn the guest rooms. The inn's hearty breakfasts might include "piggy pudding" (rich pastry over sausage) and herbed egg-and-tomato pie.

St. Petersburg★★

105 mi southwest of Orlando. Take I-4 West to I-275 South.
Tourist information: 727-464-7200 or 877-352-3224; www.floridasbeach.com.

Sunny St. Petersburg is Tampa on holiday. Lying on the west side of Tampa Bay, St. Peter achieved resort status in the 1920s, when two world-class resorts were built here: the Vinoy Park downtown (now the Renaissance Vinoy Resort) and the Don CeSar on the beach *(see Must Stay/Tampa Bay Area)*. Today the city draws vacationers to its relaxed lifestyle, first-rate museums, sparkling Gulf beaches *(10mi west of downtown)*, 7mi of landscaped waterfront parks, and wonderful warm weather.

Salvador Dalí Museum★★★

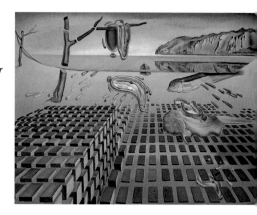

1000 Third St. S.
727-823-3767. www.salvador dalimuseum.org. Open year-round Mon–Sat 9:30am–5:30pm (Thu until 8pm) & Sun noon–5:30pm. Closed Thanksgiving Day & Dec 25. $12.50.

Your most eccentric relative probably couldn't hold a candle to Salvador Dalí, the flamboyant painter who became as famous for his skinny handlebar mustache and bold publicity stunts, as for his artistry.

The world's most comprehensive collection of works by the late Spanish Surrealist resides in this former warehouse on the St. Petersburg waterfront. Founded by Cleveland industrialist A. Reynolds Morse and his wife, Eleanor, the facility ranks as one of Florida's most popular art museums. Six galleries display pieces from the collection of 95 oil paintings, more than 100 water-colors and drawings, and 1,300 graphics, sculptures, photographs and art objects.

Dalí's Masterworks on Display
• *Nature Morte Vivante* (1956)
• *Velazquez Painting the Infanta Margarita with the Lights and Shadows of His Own Glory* (1958)
• *The Discovery of America by Christopher Columbus* (1958-59)
• *The Ecumenical Council* (1960)
• *The Hallucinogenic Toreador* (1969-70)
• *Portrait of My Dead Brother* (1963)
• *Galacidalacidesoxiribonucleicacid (Homage to Crick and Watson)* (1965)

Hello, Dalí

Born and raised in a Catalonian farming village near Barcelona, **Salvador Dalí** (1904–1989) began painting at a young age. He attended the San Fernando Academy of Fine Arts in Madrid and held his first one-man show in Barcelona in 1925 at age 21. In 1929 he moved to France, where he joined the Paris Surrealist Group, who believed in the power of dreams. Also in that year, he met Gala Eluard, his future wife and the inspiration for much of his work. Dalí soon became one of the Surrealist's brash leaders, painting such subjects as time, sex and death in obsessive detail.

By 1940 however, Dalí had broken with the group and returned to "Classical" painting, as embodied in the High Renaissance works of Raphael. The artist executed his symbolic and trompe l'œil effects in 18 **masterworks**—huge canvases dealing with historical, scientific or religious themes—each of which took at least a year to complete.

Museum of Fine Arts★

255 Beach Dr. NE. 727-896-2667. www.fine-arts.org. Open year-round Tues–Sat 10am–5pm, Sun 1pm–5pm. Closed Mon & major holidays. $8.

All 20 galleries in this attractive Palladian-style building are housed on one floor. Opened in 1965, the Museum of Fine Arts presents a wide-ranging permanent collection, covering the centuries from antiquities and world masterpieces to contemporary works. Among the 4,000 works, you'll find 19C and 20C French Impressionist paintings, early Asian art, and a luminous collection of **Steuben glass**. In the category of American art, **Georgia O'Keeffe**'s glorious painting, *Poppy* (1927), is considered one of the most important works in the museum's collection.

The Pier★

East end of 2nd Ave. NE. 727-821-6443. www.stpete-pier.com. Open year-round Mon–Thu 10am–9pm, Fri & Sat 10am–10pm, & Sun 11am–7pm.

An upside-down pyramid? That's what you'll find at the end of St. Petersburg's downtown pier. Opened in 1973, the modernistic Pier with its bright blue roof juts a quarter of a mile into Tampa Bay. The five-story structure contains an information desk and restaurants and shops on the first level, the **Pier Aquarium** *(free)* on the second level, and a restaurant and observation deck on the top. Here you can also fish, rent surrey bikes and sailboats, or sign up for a cruise on the *Dolphin Queen*.

Living Large on St. Pete Beach

The powder-white sand beaches of St. Petersburg and **Clearwater** are considered by connoisseurs to be among the best on the planet. No wonder, then, that many beach-goers flock to St. Petersburg Beach. A resort town of nearly 10,000 souls, St. Pete Beach anchors the southern end of Gulf Boulevard, which stretches 18mi north to Clearwater, a popular strand on Florida's Gulf coast. Though not a scenic drive, the highway passes many beach access points sandwiched between motels and condominiums. The beach itself offers clean, whisper-soft sand and gentle Gulf waters. (Plan to pay for parking at public-access areas.) The town is the setting for the historic **Don CeSar Beach Resort and Spa**, a pink palace that attracts the rich and famous *(see Must Stay/Tampa Bay Area)*. A few blocks from the hotel sits the **Nancy Markhoe Gallery** *(3112 Pass a Grill Way; 727-360-0729)*, a shop filled with high-quality handmade jewelry, pottery and glassworks by American craftspeople.

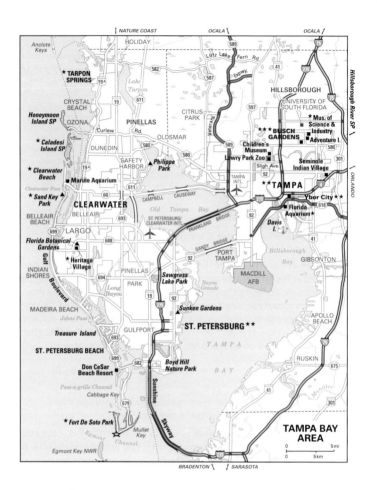

Tampa★★

Tampa is located 84mi southwest of Orlando. Follow I-4 West to I-275 South and take Exit 44 to downtown Tampa. Tampa Bay Convention & Visitors Bureau is located at 400 N. Tampa St.; 813-223-1111 or 800-448-2672; www.visittampabay.com.

Bustling modern city, cruise port, vacation destination. Florida's third-largest city is all these things and more. Blessed with fine weather year-round and an enviable setting on the blue waters of Tampa Bay (Florida's biggest open-water estuary) Tampa offers a host of attractions for all ages. Busch Gardens, the Florida Aquarium and the Museum of Science and Industry can keep kids busy for days, while the beaches of nearby Clearwater and St. Petersburg and the frenetic night-club scene of Ybor City will satisfy teens and their parents.

Downtown Tampa's once-sleepy waterfront has been revived with the state-of-the-art Ice Palace hockey arena; the Garrison Seaport Center, (which includes the Florida Aquarium and the city's busy cruise terminals); and **Channelside** *(next to Florida Aquarium; 813-223-4250; www.channelsidetampa.com)*, a complex of restaurants, clubs, boutiques, and a 3-D IMAX cinema.

Busch Gardens Tampa Bay★★★

8mi northeast of downtown Tampa at 3000 E. Busch Blvd. 813-987-5090 or 800-372-1797. www.buschgardens.com. Open year-round daily; hours vary. $51.95 adults, $42.95 children (ages 3-9).

Yes, it's another theme park—in case you didn't get enough of them in Orlando. This one's brought to you by the local Busch family, who built a brewery just south of the University of South Florida in 1959 and opened a bird sanctuary on the grounds. The simple venture mushroomed into the internationally famous zoo/amusement park that reigns today as the queen of Tampa attractions. Tied to an African theme, Busch Gardens incorporates nearly 3,000 animals and 300 acres of tropical gardens, as well as roller coasters, thrill rides, music and shows. Here's how it all breaks down:

Bird Gardens – In **Lory Landing** aviary, an enclosed rain forest setting allows parrots, lorikeets, hornbills and other tropical birds to fly freely. Be sure to catch a **Bird Show** featuring trained raptors and parrots.

The Congo – Be sure you come to The Congo on an empty stomach: This is the home of some of the Southeast's most high-octane **roller coasters**. **Kumba**, one of the largest and fastest (60mph), zooms riders through seven inversions; the 1,200ft-long **Python** sends you through two 360-degree loops; and **Gwazi**, billed as Florida's first dueling—or double—wooden roller coaster, spirals riders along 7,000ft of track in two simultaneously operating trains. If coasters aren't your thing, brave the whitewater of **Congo River Rapids** in a 12-person raft. At Claw Island, rare Bengal tigers roam a jungle habitat.

Edge of Africa – Introduced on video by animal handler Jack Hanna, Edge of Africa lets you get as close to baboons, hippos, lions and hyenas as acrylic panes will allow.

Egypt –The easternmost area of Busch Gardens holds nearly seven acres of rides, including **Montu**, a spine-tingling inverted roller coaster, and **Akbar's Adventure Tours**, a simulated journey around the pyramids and into a haunted tomb.

Adventure Island

Adjacent to Busch Gardens, entrance on McKinley Ave. 813-987-5600. www.adventureisland.com. Open year-round daily 9am, closing times vary. $29.95 adults, $27.95 children). If you worked up a sweat standing in lines at Busch Gardens, this 30-acre water park is the place to cool off. And in case you thought a water park would be relaxing, be forewarned that more thrills await you here. Launch yourself through 230ft of intertwined tubes on Caribbean Corkscrew; hurl your body down the 210ft Gulf Scream waterslide at speeds of 25mph; or jump from a 20ft-high platform into Paradise Lagoon. Whatever your pleasure, everything here ends with a splash. (Parents, never fear—the park has more than 50 certified lifeguards to supervise the water activities.)

Morocco – An ice show in Africa? Sure, why not? Anything can happen in this bustling marketplace with its mysterious tiled palace. There's also a bakery, an open-air dining room and two theaters presenting musical revues.

Nairobi – Feel like monkeying around? In **Myombe Reserve**, a three-acre gorilla and chimpanzee habitat, you can observe primates up-close through a glass window. From Nairobi station, the steam-powered **Trans-Veldt Railroad** carries visitors around the park in open coaches.

Serengeti Plain – From antelopes to zebras, more than 700 large African animals roam in herds on this 29-acre grassy savanna. For long-distance viewing, take the skyride or train, but for a closer vantage point try the flatbed trucks of the **Serengeti Safari** tours.

Stanleyville – Water rules in this replica African village. Here you'll find the **Stanley Falls Log Flume** and the **Tanganyika Tidal Wave**, a ride that creates a huge splash as it careens down a 55ft drop. Stanleyville Theatre and Zambezi Pavilion both feature live entertainment.

Timbuktu – In this re-created desert trading center, you'll find the **Scorpion** roller coaster that drops 62ft into a 360-degree loop. In the **Dolphin Theatre**, leaping dolphins and a comical California sea lion steal the show.

Museum of Science & Industry★★

4801 E. Fowler Ave. 813-987-6100 or 800-995-MOSI. www.mosi.org. Open year-round daily Mon–Fri 9am–5pm, Sat & Sun 9am–7pm. $14.95.

Ready to improve your mind? This classic, hands-on science museum can teach you a thing or two. In 1995 MOSI jumped back to the future with the addition of its starkly modern, four-story, aluminum-clad West Wing, which now houses the museum's main exhibit area. A roster of changing special exhibitions complements the 450 permanent displays. On your way to the museum entrance, stop at the **BioWorks Butterfly Garden** for a glimpse of the brightly colored creatures and to discover how water in natural wetlands cleans itself.

Attention, Dinophiles: MOSI is one of only a few museums in the world to display the diplodocus dinosaurs, among the largest dinosaurs ever discovered. Look for these three-story-high sauropods in the lobby—you can't miss them!

Making the Most of MOSI

- **Gulf Coast Hurricane** – Experience 74mph hurricane-force winds and learn how to prepare for tropical storms.
- **350-seat IMAX Dome Theatre** – Watch a changing line-up of films play on an 82ft-high screen.
- **Our Place on the Planet** – Explore Florida's unique flora, fauna and geography in the context of an ordinary backyard.
- **Amazing You** – Watch a bicycle-riding skeleton to see how your muscles move, and find out why you should eat your peas, at the Food for Thought Cafe.
- **Our Place in the Universe** – Meet planet Earth and its solar system.
- **Saunders Planetarium** – *3rd floor, East Wing.* Peer into space through the museum's high-powered telescopes.

Florida Aquarium★

701 Channelside Dr. at Garrison Seaport Center. 813-273-4000. www.flaquarium.org. Open year-round daily 9:30am–5pm. Closed Thanksgiving Day & Dec 25. $15.

Is something fishy in Tampa? You bet there is—it's the Florida Aquarium. Beneath a soaring green glass dome, the aquarium harbors more than a million gallons of fresh- and saltwater that support 10,000 aquatic plants and animals. Go with the flow, and follow a drop of water from its underground source to the ocean. Viewing galleries are laid out in four aquatic communities:

Wetlands – Amid humid habitats of cypress swamps, mangrove forests and saw grass marshes you'll find river otters, roseate spoonbills, alligators, fresh-water bass, white ibis, great horned owls and other creatures.

Bays and Beaches – Ecosystems include bay bottoms, with graceful stingrays and floor-dwelling guitarfish. See if you can spot the bonnethead shark or the spiny lobster.

Coral Reef – Colorful butterfly fish dart through forests of staghorn coral and sharks lurk in dark grottoes. You'll peer through a 14ft-high transparent wall for glimpses of 60 species of tropical fish. Housed in a 500,000-gallon tank, the exhibit is modeled after the coral formations of the Dry Tortugas that lie off the Florida Keys.

Sea Hunt – Mysterious creatures of the deep sea—scorpion fish, dragon moray eels and the giant Pacific octopus—are on display here. Stand nose-to-nose with the toothsome predators of Shark Bay, and watch divers get close-up and personal with sharks during twice-daily shark shows.

Who's Who of Early Tampa

Henry Bradley Plant – Visionary transportation tycoon who brought the railroad to Tampa in 1884 and assured the city's future as a trade center. Plant's Tampa Bay Hotel, which opened in 1891, attracted luminaries from around the globe.

Vicente Martinez Ybor – Key West entrepreneur who relocated his cigar manufacturing business to town in 1886, making Tampa the "Cigar Capital of the World" in the late 19C.

Ybor City★★

Ybor City, 1.6mi from downtown Tampa, is about 84mi southwest of Orlando. Take I-4 West to Ybor City exit. Ybor City Chamber of Commerce operates a visitor center at 180 E. 9th Ave.; 813-248-3712; www.ybor.org.

Looking for nightlife? Trendy Ybor City (pronounced EE-bore) is Tampa's Latin-accented hotspot for nightlife and local color. The heart of Tampa's Cuban population once beat within this one-square-mile National Historic Landmark District, the center of Tampa's cigar-making industry in the 19C. Thanks to a resurgence of interest in Ybor City, buildings have been renovated and historical elements (cobblestone streets, Old World street lamps, wrought-iron balconies) spruced up, as Ybor City has evolved into one of the city's hippest nightspots.

The district is named for cigar manufacturer and Cuban exile **Vicente Martinez Ybor**, who chose Tampa as the new base for his operations when labor-union pressures in Key West forced him to relocate his business in the late 19C. Ybor's cigar factory opened in 1886 and soon became the largest in the world. Sadly, the advent of machine-rolled cigars, the increasing popularity of cigarettes, and the beginning of the Depression spelled doom for the hand-rolled cigar industry in Ybor City. Now produced by machine, local cigars generate $150 million in annual sales revenue.

Café Creole – *1320-1330 9th Ave.* With its graceful arches, Café Creole gained fame as the Cherokee Club, a rowdy hotel that opened in 1888. In its heyday, the hotel welcomed Cuban revolutionary José Martí, presidents Teddy Roosevelt and Grover Cleveland and Sir Winston Churchill.

Centro Ybor – *16th St. between 7th & 9th Aves. www.centroybor.com.* Central Espanol, formerly a mutual-aid society, has been renovated as the cornerstone of a $45 million complex that includes restaurants, shops, a comedy club, a high-tech entertainment center and a multiscreen movie theater, set around an open-air plaza.

Columbia Restaurant – *7th Ave. at 21st St. 813-248-4961. www.columbiarestaurant.com.* A landmark since 1905, Florida's oldest restaurant, encompasses an entire block and is admired for its colorful exterior tile work.

Seventh Avenue –
This is *the* place to go
in Ybor City. A walk
along the neighbor-
hood's main thorough-
fare reveals some of
its interesting archi-
tecture, as well as
some of its best
restaurants and clubs.
Seventh Avenue takes
on a Mardi Gras atmo-
sphere on Thursday,
Friday and Saturday

nights, when police close the street to traffic *(between 13th & 20th Sts.)* and
Seventh Avenue becomes a hopping pedestrian promenade.

Ybor City State Museum – *1818 9th Ave. 813-247-6323. www.ybormuseum.org.
Open year-round daily 9am–5pm. Closed major holidays. $2.* Housed in the
1923 yellow-brick Ferlita Bakery building, the museum outlines the development of Ybor City from frontier village to its recent renaissance. Guided tours
of **La Casita** provide a peek at a typical late-19C cigar maker's cottage.

Club-Hopping in Ybor City

Want to party like it's 1999? Ybor City offers so many options, you'll never get
y-bored. The Ybor City Chamber of Commerce offers a printed guide to party palaces
(visit their office at 1600 E. 8th Ave.). Here are some possibilities; note that clubs
change their styles as often as Madonna does, so call before you visit.

The Amphitheater – *1609 E. 7th Ave. 813-248-2331. www.amphitheaterybor.com.*
Touring DJs spin techno and rave music at this entertainment complex.

The Blue Shark – *1620 7th Ave. 813-248-3499.* Live blues acts entertain in this main-
stream club.

Carmine's – *1802 7th Ave. 813-248-3834.* It's an Italian/Spanish restaurant by day, patio
bar by night, with DJ-driven 70s funk and disco.

Club Hedo – *1510 E. 7th Ave. 813-248-4336. www.clubhedo.com.* Dance to edgy hip-
hop and some Top 40s tunes, spun by a DJ.

Club Prana – *1619 E. 7th Ave. 813-241-4139. www.clubprana.com.* The trendy, five-level
club features DJs spinning hip-hop, glass dance floors and a VIP room, "The Sanctuary."

Empire Club – *1902 E. 7th Ave. 813-263-2657. www.empirelive.com.* A youngish crowd
dances under the strobe lights here to techno, hip-hop and ska.

Green Iguana Bar & Grill – *1708 E. 7th Ave. 813-248-9555. www.greeniguana.net.* This
one bills itself as Tampa's only beach bar, but it's not on the beach. Live music and a
casual ambience consistently draw crowds.

The Rare Olive – *1601 E. 7th Ave. 813-248-2333. www.partybor.com.* This upscale martini and cigar bar draws an older crowd and offers live music—jazz, reggae, funk—
dancing, and signature martinis.

Twilight – *1507 7th Ave. 813-247-4225. www.twighlightnightclub.com.* The Deco-style
room offers a great sound system, an upstairs balcony and live music that runs the
gamut from alternative to punk.

Tarpon Springs★

31mi northwest of Tampa on Florida's Gulf Coast. From Tampa, take Rte. 580 West to US-19 North. US-19 will lead you into Tarpon Springs. From Orlando, take I-275 North to I-75 North, then take Rte. 56 to Tarpon Springs. Rte. 56 turns into Rte. 54. Take Rte. 54 to US-19 South and follow it into town. Visitor information: 727-937-6109 or www.tarponsprings.com.

Call it "Little Greece." A surprising taste of the Mediterranean flavors this small town on Florida's west coast, about two hours west of Orlando. Best known as a commercial sponging center, Tarpon Springs is home to a strong, close-knit Greek community centered around the sponge docks on the Anclote River, an estuary of the Gulf of Mexico.

Sponge beds were discovered in the area in the 1870s, and soon Tarpon Springs overtook Key West as the hub of the sponge trade in Florida. A few years later, the town blossomed as a winter resort and health spa, when wealthy "snowbirds" built Victorian houses and bungalows here. Beginning in 1905, expert sponge divers—most of whom came from the Dodecanese Islands near Crete—immigrated from Greece. The Tarpon Springs sponge business peaked in the 1930s. By the late 1940s, a local blight, America's preference for synthetic sponges, and growing Mediterranean competition destroyed the Florida market. In 1986, however, the Soviet nuclear-reactor disaster in Chernobyl wiped out the Mediterranean beds, and Tarpon Springs came bouncing back to be the largest natural sponge market in the world—with annual revenues of $7 million.

Reasons to Stroll Dodecanese Boulevard

Running parallel to the Anclote River (north of Tarpon Ave., off N. Pinellas Ave./US-19A), this waterfront thoroughfare is where it's at.

- To get a sense of this lively Greek community.
- To poke through bins of sponges and curios from the sea.
- To visit colorful family-run cafes and bakeries for tastes of honey-soaked baklava and other Greek specialties that scent the air.
- To explore the side streets behind the boulevard, where the atmosphere recalls the residents' homeland.
- To see the working shrimp and sponge boats that are tied up at the main dock near the east end of the boulevard.
- To take a cruise aboard one of the traditional sponging vessels and see a demonstration of sponge harvesting.
- To visit the former **Sponge Exchange** (no. 735), which now houses specialty shops and displays an early-20C sponge-diving boat in its plaza.
- To touch stingrays and baby sand sharks at the **Tarpon Springs Aquarium** (no. 850, west end of sponge docks; 727-938-5378).

Sponge Diving

A primitive aquatic animal with no brain or nervous system (not exactly the life of the party!), the natural sponge (phylum Porifera) can be found in all seas but prefers shallow, temperate waters. Living in colonies at depths ranging from several feet to 28,000ft, sponges attach to stationary objects, such as rocks and coral, on the sea floor. In shallow water, divers can collect these from a boat using a long-handled metal hook. In deeper water, divers must walk along the bottom (sponges can be harvested from depths up to 150ft) and hook the sponges by hand, walking at a 45-degree angle against the current. Attached by air-hose to their boat, Tarpon Springs divers use the same type of rubberized suit, round copper helmet and iron boots introduced by the first crew of Greek spongers who arrived in 1905. This equipment is quite a load—altogether it weighs 172 pounds.

After the sponges are gathered, they are cleaned and dried. The part of the sponge that you use is actually the animal's skeleton, which is composed of a fine meshwork of fibrous spongin—a material related to horn—that can absorb 25 times its weight in water.

While there are more than 4,500 known species of natural sponges, only four with any commercial value live in the Gulf of Mexico:

- wool (the best grade, used for car and bath sponges)
- yellow (household sponges)
- wire (packing and insulation)
- grass (cosmetic sponges)

You'll find all these for sale in Tarpon Springs, along with decorative finger sponges and loofahs—actually a land-growing member of the cucumber family (who knew?).

Must Eat: Orlando Area Restaurants

The venues listed below were selected for their ambience, location and/or value for money. Rates indicate the average cost of an appetizer, an entrée and a dessert for one person (not including tax, gratuity or beverages). Most restaurants are open daily and accept major credit cards. Call for information regarding reservations, dress code and opening hours. Restaurants listed are located in Orlando, unless otherwise noted. For a complete list of restaurants mentioned in this guide, see Index.

$$$$ over $50	**$$** $15–$30
$$$ $30–$50	**$** under $15

Luxury

Atlantis $$$$ Seafood

Renaissance Orlando Resort, 6677 Sea Harbor Dr. Dinner only. 407-351-5555. www.renaissancehotels.com.

Mahogany panels with etched-glass inserts provide diners with a sense of intimacy here, enhanced by music from a harpist (listen closely and you'll notice songs from pop stars like Shakira). Diners can see the evening's entrées—poached sea bass or shrimp in puff pastry—before they choose. Chef Mitsuo Miyashita varies the menu nightly, but he always offers dessert soufflés made to order.

Emeril's $$$$ Cajun-Creole

Universal Studios CityWalk, 6000 Universal Blvd. 407-224-2424. www.emerils.com/restaurants/orlando.

New Orleans celebrity chef Emeril Lagasse brought his flair and his wonderful cooking to Orlando in 1999. His restaurant has been standing room only almost ever since. Insiders sometimes take dinner at the bar because it beats the reservations backlog. Emeril is only in town on an average of once a month, so chef Barnard Carmouche holds the fort for him, serving up Cajun-Creole specialties and toothsome sweets like chocolate soufflé with Grand Marnier, fresh berries and hot chocolate sauce. In the cellar some 12,000 bottles await uncorking.

Moderate

California Grill

$$$ Eclectic

Contemporary Resort, Walt Disney World. 407-939-3463. www.disneyworld.com.

Considered to be the best restaurant at Walt Disney World, the California Grill has won many awards with chef Clifford Pleau at the helm—it was even rated "Top Meal in America" by *USA Today*. An open kitchen is the centerpiece of this restaurant-in-the-round: Watch chefs roll sushi, toss pizza, pipe pastry and stuff Sonoma goat cheese into ravioli. Grilled tuna is the top seller here, but the sushi wins raves, as does the lemongrass risotto with grilled shrimp.

Charlie's Lobster House

$$$ Seafood

8445 International Dr. Dinner only. 407-352-6929. www.charlieslobsterhouse.com.

This elegant Mercado Village restaurant prepares fresh local seafood as you like it—grilled, sautéed or broiled. Regulars know to select from the chef's daily specials, such as blackened tuna with herb hollandaise and citrus-glazed barbecued black grouper. Natural wood wainscoting and planters hanging from the 15ft ceiling create a relaxed setting. Save room for the cheesecake with fresh berry sauce.

Chatham's Place

$$$ Continental

7575 Dr. Phillips Blvd. Dinner only. 407-345-2992. www.chathamsplace.com.

This intimate, privately owned restaurant is a comfortable change from all the city's theme-park hoopla. The smiling staff is friendly, and they do a fine job with the restaurant's signature dish, black Florida grouper slathered in pecan butter. The rack of lamb au jus and baked jumbo shrimp also earn raves—in fact, Chatham's routinely gets high marks from its patrons.

Coral Reef Restaurant $$$ Seafood

The Living Seas Pavilion at Epcot. 407-939-3463. www.disneyworld.com.

A cool oasis inside Epcot, this dining room is bathed in dreamlike blue light, with the left side devoted to a floor-to-ceiling saltwater aquarium. Gaze at the 500-pound grouper as you wait for your meal—perhaps a mixed shellfish grill, pan-smoked grouper, or Maine lobster pie. The Coral Reef is a bit pricier than some of the other options here, but the just-flown-in catch, simply but wonderfully prepared, is worth the splurge.

Dux $$$ Continental

Peabody Orlando Hotel, 9801 International Dr. Dinner only. 407-345-4550. www.peabodyorlando.com.

Named after the fowl that parade through the hotel's lobby each day, this acclaimed restaurant is a favorite of local foodies. Decorated in tones of copper, bronze and gold with paintings of the hotel's cherished mascots, the dining room is worthy of special occasions. The food lives up to the billing, a sparkling marriage of American favorites spiked with exotic touches. The bone-in filet mignon with Roquefort tempts many a diner, as does the Bailey's Irish crème brulée. The menu changes to reflect seasonal ingredients.

Le Coq au Vin $$$ French

4800 S. Orange Ave. 407-851-6980. www.lecoqauvin.com.

This small, unpretentious restaurant serves some of the best French food in central Florida. It's the place where rival chefs dine on their days off. Louis Perrotte supervises the kitchen, while his wife Magdalena welcomes guests. The dining spot is named for its most popular, and least expensive, dish—chicken stewed in red wine. More daring diners opt for the braised rabbit.

Wolfgang Puck's Café $$$ International

Downtown Disney West Side, Lake Buena Vista. Dinner only in second-floor dining room. 407-938-9653. www.downtowndisney.com.

This isn't one restaurant, it's a quartet. There's a casual cafe and a lively sushi bar downstairs and a quick takeaway counter next door. Upstairs is Puck's famed fine-dining establishment. Although the celebrated chef has closed his renowned Spago's in Hollywood, California, it seems as if the place has been reborn here in Orlando. Tiles and polished wood are featured in the décor. Kitchens are open, so patrons can see their signature pizzas being twirled and baked in the brick oven. Virtually every dish involves an imaginative fusion of American, Asian and European ingredients.

Budget

Bongo's Cuban Café
$$ Cuban

Downtown Disney West Side, Lake Buena Vista. 407-828-0999. www.bongoscubancafe.com.

Owned by pop star Gloria Estefan and hubby Emilio, this Latin-flavored restaurant boasts good eats and fabulous mojitos, but it's the lively vibe that really makes the place jump. Nab a spot on the patio alongside Seven Seas Lagoon and watch the passing parade (which gets really lively around 10pm).

Flying Fish Café
$$ Seafood

Disney's BoardWalk, Lake Buena Vista. Dinner only. 407-939-2359. www.disneyworld.com.

It's worth a trip to Disney's re-created Atlantic City (c.1930s) to check out this lively spot with its Ferris wheel motif and bustling open kitchen. The menu relies chiefly on fresh seafood and seasonal fruits and veggies. Chefs ham it up while slinging grits alongside grilled quail—plus, they serve a killer lava cake with erupting white chocolate.

Harvey's Bistro
$$ American

390 N. Orange Ave. 407-246-6560. www.harveysbistro.com.

Comfort food with a modern slant keeps residents coming back to this stylish eatery inside downtown's Bank of America building. Hearty entrées include pot roast in burgundy gravy, and roast duck with strawberry sauce. Lighter appetites will favor the day's catch. Dark-wood paneling, black-and-white marble floors, and mirror-lined walls give the buzzing dining room a chic, yet casual look.

House of Blues
$$ Southern

Downtown Disney West Side, Lake Buena Vista. 407-934-2583. www.hob.com.

Unless you've got an HOB outpost in your own town, you owe yourself a visit to this roll-up-your-sleeves, grab-a-pile-o'-napkins place. The Southern comfort food—prepared with a contemporary slant—is earthy and delicious. A dose of their jambalaya with dirty rice or fiery crawfish etoufée, along with bread pudding drenched in Bourbon sauce will cure the baddest case of the blues. The famed Sunday gospel brunch features live gospel acts.

Mama Della's Ristorante
$$ Italian

Portofino Bay Hotel, Universal Blvd. 407-224-9255. www.universalorlando.com.

This hotel replicates its namesake Italian city with amazing authenticity, so it makes sense that they maintain the same high standards in their kitchen. And so they do, both here and at their pricier restaurant, **Delfino Riviera ($$$)**. Go to Mama's if you've got a craving for chicken cacciatore and a nice cannoli for dessert. Mama Della herself presides over the place as though it was her own home, complete with mismatched china, and pasta served in heaping bowls.

Ming Court
$$ Chinese

9188 International Dr. 407-351-9988. www.ming-court.com.

There's the typical Chinese take-out joint, then there's Ming Court, an elegant, upscale take on Chinese food. Voted "Best Chinese Food" by the readers of *Orlando* magazine, Ming Court offers everything from really good dim sum and sushi to aged steaks. A sprawling place, it tends to attract a slew of big parties (conventioneers from the nearby Convention Center) in the evening, so your best bet is to come for lunch or an early dinner.

Straub's
$$ Seafood

5101 E. Colonial Dr. Dinner only. 407-273-9330.

Chef-owner Rob Straub has built an international reputation with his fresh mahi mahi, Florida lobster tail, and salmon steak marinated in lime juice, spices and honey. Ask the wait staff for suggestions because they know what's fresh. All the fish is prepared to order; insiders prefer their fish grilled or broiled, not the traditional deep-fried.

White Wolf Café
$$ International

1829 N. Orange Ave. 407-895-5590. www.whitewolfcafe.com.

Located in the heart of Orlando's Antique Row, this bistro is named for the owner's white German shepherd. The storefront started life as an antique shop, with a few snacks being served to bring in customers and give the local trade a place to relax. Gradually the food took over. Tables and chairs moved in, knickknacks moved out. The eclectic fare runs the gamut from mahi-mahi with mango Thai chile sauce to pork tenderloin stuffed with apples and walnuts to quiche and lasagne.

NBA City
$ American

Universal Studios CityWalk, 6000 Universal Blvd. 407-363-5919. www.nbacity.com.

Play basketball skill games and test your knowledge of roundball trivia while you wait (and you will wait) for a table here. Once inside, sit in a semicircle around a humongous video screen and watch great moments in hoop history. The food—inexpensive by CityWalk standards—is better than you'd expect; it's an All-American mix of grilled chicken, pasta, salads, sandwiches and killer milkshakes.

Thai Place
$ Thai

501 N. Orlando Ave., Winter Park. 407-644-8449. www.thethaiplace.com.

This small restaurant is decorated with a black ceiling painted with artwork, similar to ceilings found in native Thai homes. Curries here include red, green, yellow and peanut, all made from different pastes and laced with fresh herbs and spices. Beware, though—the kitchen staff can produce some dishes that may overwhelm your palate while bringing tears to your eyes. Try the *pla lad prik* (whole fish baked with spices in red bell peppers) for a taste you won't forget. Thai spring rolls, crispier and spicier than their Chinese cousins, come with a tangy peanut dipping sauce.

Dining in the Tampa Bay Area

Moderate

Bern's Steak House $$$ American

1208 Howard Ave., Tampa. Dinner only. 813-251-2421. www.bernssteakhouse.com.

This Tampa institution offers meat connoisseurs six different cuts of aged US Prime beef, from chateaubriand to T-bone, served with garlic butter, soup, salad, baked potato and home-grown vegetables. The encyclopedic wine list boasts nearly 8,000 entries. Gilded plaster columns, red wallpaper and murals depicting French vineyards set the mood for a memorable dining experience. Order your dessert by phone in one of the many glass-encased booths upstairs.

Hurricane Seafood Restaurant $$$ Seafood

807 Gulf Way, St. Petersburg Beach. 727-360-9558. www.thehurricane.com.

For decades, this popular 498-seat beachfront bar, restaurant and nightclub has been *the* place to watch the area's dazzling sunsets. From the rooftop deck of the third floor, beachgoers and business types alike enjoy drinks and 360 degrees of gulf, mainland and bay. The seafood matches the view, especially the local favorite, flaky saltwater grouper served grilled, broiled, blackened or fried. After the first-floor cafe closes at 1am, the second-floor dining room becomes a late-night dance club.

Budget

Columbia $$ Spanish

2117 E. 7th Ave., Ybor City. 813-248-4961. www.columbiarestaurant.com.

Encompassing an entire block within Tampa's historic district, Florida's oldest operating restaurant (1905), still family-owned, is a bastion of Old World charm and Spanish-Cuban cuisine. Linen tablecloths, gracious service and hand-painted tiles set the scene for tapas, gazpacho and Columbia's signature *paella a la Valenciana*, the national dish of Spain. Choose a vintage label from the house cellar or try the freshly made fruit-filled sangria. Nightly *(except Sun)*, flamenco dancers leave patrons tapping their toes.

Skipper's Smokehouse and Oyster Bar $$ Seafood

910 Skipper Rd., Tampa. 813-971-0666. www.skipperssmokehouse.com.

The weather-beaten walkways and overturned boats fronting this landmark restaurant belie its offshore location. Inside, the atmosphere is definitely beach style: laid back and low key. Seating is limited and the tiny oyster bar fills up fast, but overflow crowds can dine on alligator chili, garlic crab, and steamed mud bugs (crawfish) under the stars at picnic tables outside. Reggae, blues and zydeco musicians perform nightly beneath the Skipperdome's thatched awning.

The properties listed below were selected for their ambience, location and/or value for money. Prices reflect the average cost for a standard double room for two people (not including applicable taxes). Hotels in Orlando constantly offer special discount packages. Price ranges quoted do not reflect the Florida hotel tax of 11%. Properties are located in Orlando, unless otherwise specified. For a list of hotels described in this guide, see Index.

$$$$$	over $300	$$	$75–$125
$$$$	$200–$300	$	less than $75
$$$	$125–$200		

Luxury

Disney's Animal Kingdom Lodge $$$$ 1,293 rooms

2901 Osceola Pkwy., Bay Lake. 407-934-7639. www.disneyworld.com.

When booking a reservation at this horseshoe-shaped lodge, ask for a Savanna View room, which offers vistas of Animal Kingdom's grazing animals from its private balcony. Bring binoculars and a zoom camera, because some creatures come within 30ft. Decorated with African spears and masks, the lobby has a stream running through it and a huge mud fireplace. Enjoy breakfast in Boma—Flavors of Africa, a family restaurant, and later stop for Kenyan coffee in the Victoria Falls Lounge.

Disney's Fort Wilderness Resort $$$$ 406 cabins

4510 Fort Wilderness Trail, Lake Buena Vista. 407-824-2900. www.disneyworld.com. Campsites also available ($).

The ultimate in resort self-catering, this collection of log houses and cabins is complemented by campsites designed for pitching tents or hooking up trailers and mobile homes. Outdoor grills are plentiful and activities range from hay and pony rides to volleyball, biking, fishing and basketball; youngsters especially will enjoy the petting farm. Nightlife centers on a a nightly musical review, where ticket holders enjoy an all-you-can-eat feast and sing-alongs.

Disney's Grand Floridian Resort & Spa

$$$$ 900 rooms

4401 Grand Floridian Way, Lake Buena Vista. 407-824-3000. www.disneyworld.com.

Disney's most luxurious property is a Victorian-era waterside complex set on 40 acres along Magic Kingdom's monorail route. The flagship resort's five-story lobby—with carved moldings, an aviary and an open-cage elevator—is topped by illuminated stained-glass domes. Elegant guest rooms feature dark woodwork and old-fashioned sink fittings. While parents are enjoying the full-service spa, kids can frolic at the Mouseketeer Club. The French-inspired menu at **Citrico's** (**$$$**) includes the signature braised veal shank.

Hard Rock Hotel

$$$$ 650 rooms

5800 Universal Blvd. 800-BE-A-STAR. www.hardrock.com.

Among Universal's three on-site resort hotels, this is *the* place to stay for families with teens. You'll know you've entered Cooldom when you see the fountain made of 42 bronze guitars! Filled with an impressive collection of rock 'n' roll memorabilia, the hotel has a 12,000sq ft swimming pool with a water slide, and five restaurants (including the Hard Rock Café). The Hard Rock is a just short stroll away from Universal's Islands of Adventure park and CityWalk.

The Peabody Orlando

$$$$ 891 rooms

9801 International Dr. 407-352-4000 or 800-PEABODY. www.peabodyorlando.com.

The eastern outpost of Memphis' original Peabody is in the Plaza International district. Potted palms, bamboo furnishings and a two-story waterfall fill the lobby atrium. Twice a day the red carpet is rolled out for the resident ducks to march to the marble fountain. Pale woods and pastels extend the hotel's tropical theme to the spacious bedrooms. Venerable **Dux** *(see Must Eat)* restaurant envelops diners in its signature waterfowl motif.

Portofino Bay Hotel
$$$$ 750 rooms

5601 Universal Blvd. 407-503-1000 or 888-837-2273. www.universalorlando.com.

Operated by the Loews Corp. on Universal theme-park property, this colorful five-floor hotel edges a large body of water like the bayside Italian fishing village for which it is named. Tile roofs slant out over wrought-iron balconies and many rooms overlook a cobblestone piazza. Rooms are spacious, with four-poster beds, duvets, armoires and marble-accented bathrooms. All guests are admitted to Universal parks an hour before the general public via water taxi across the lagoon.

Moderate

Disney's Coronado Springs Resort
$$$ 1,967 rooms

1000 W. Buena Vista Dr., Lake Buena Vista. 407-828-1818. www.disneyworld.com.

Among Disney's moderately priced hotels, the Southwest-themed Coronado Springs Resort stands out as an appealing option. Set near Disney-MGM Studios and the Animal Kingdom, this colorful property features Mickey Mouse-shaped cacti, a 15-acre, man-made lagoon, and two- and three-story earthy Western-style "ranchos," brightly-hued "casitas" and quirky beach "cabanas." A towering pyramid forms the splashy centerpiece of the pool/waterslide area.

Eo Inn & Urban Spa
$$$ 21 rooms

227 N. Eola Dr. 407-481-8485 or 888-481-8488. www.eoinn.com.

Overlooking Lake Eola in Thornton Park, this upscale boutique hotel operates within a recently remodeled 1923 building. Luxurious guest quarters are electronically equipped to serve as a workplace around the clock. The third floor boasts a rooftop terrace where guests can soak up Florida sunshine; continental breakfasts are also served here. Open to the public, the full-service day spa is up top as well.

Holiday Inn Family Suites Resort
$$$ 800 rooms

14500 Continental Gateway, Lake Buena Vista. 407-387-5437. www.hifamilysuites.com.

Located practically on Disney's doorstep (thus, priced slightly higher than the company's Sunspree resort), this all-suite property sports a train-station motif. There's even a teddy bear dressed as a conductor, hugging kids and signing autographs. Each suite features separate rooms for the small fry, with bunk or twin beds, and a pull-out couch in the sitting area. A mini-refrigerator and microwave help families save money on snacks and drinks. Kids eat free all day at the restaurant here, and everybody eats free at the breakfast buffet.

Hyatt Regency Grand Cypress Resort

$$$ 750 rooms

1 Grand Cypress Blvd. 407-239-1234 or 800-233-1234. www.hyatt.com.

Check into the Grand Cypress resort and you may be too busy to make it to the theme parks. This 1,500-acre resort is a vacationer's paradise, with 45 holes of championship golf, an equestrian center, a 21-acre lake, tennis courts and racquetball. Then there's the fabulous pool area with cascading waterfalls, grottoes and a water-slide. Hot tubs are tucked away in corners and hidden under waterfalls. At lakeside, there's a sand beach where you can build castles with the kids or go for a sail. Disney parks are just a short drive away.

Orlando World Center Marriott

$$$ 1,503 rooms

8701 World Center Dr. 407-239-4200 or 800-228-9290. www.marriott.com.

This 200-acre resort is built around a mammoth high-rise hotel with a 12-story atrium lobby and glass elevator. Oversize rooms are furnished in restful pastels (no theme here) and the grounds are all tropical foliage, cool waterfalls and perfectly manicured golf fairways. (The golf club offers the highly regarded John Jacobs School of Golf). Eight tennis courts and four pools add to the "everything under one roof" appeal—plus, it's very close to Disney.

Renaissance Orlando Resort

$$$ 778 rooms

6677 Sea Harbor Dr. 407-351-5555 or 800-327-6677. www.renaissancehotels.com.

The interior of the 10-floor hotel at this massive 27-acre complex reveals a cavernous, sunlit atrium sheltering 13,000 plants, an aviary, a waterfall and a koi-filled fish pond. Across the street from SeaWorld, the Renaissance features large guest quarters, attractively done in gold, green and teak. Facilities include basketball, volleyball and lighted tennis courts.

Residence Inn SeaWorld International Center

$$$ 350 suites

1100 Westwood Blvd. 407-313-3600 or 800-331-3131. www.residenceinnseaworld.com.

Even the family pet is welcome at this pleasant, six-story all-suites hotel. Rooms in the one- and two-bedroom suites feature basic hotel décor, but, for under $200 per night, the amenities make it attractive: free shuttle to SeaWorld, Universal and Wet 'n' Wild, full kitchens, free hot breakfast buffet, a playground and sports courts. Kids even have their own poolside bar, serving pizza and ice cream. As the name implies, the property is close to SeaWorld.

Must Stay: Orlando Area Hotels

Budget

The Courtyard at Lake Lucerne
$$ 30 rooms

211 N. Lucerne Circle. 407-648-5188 or 800-444-5289. www.orlandohistoricinn.com.

Ringing a tropical courtyard, this complex of four historic residences (1893–1940) overlooks downtown's Lake Lucerne. Each one reflects the period of its heyday, from Victorian jewel-tone fabrics and sleigh beds to offbeat Art Deco suites with kitchenettes. The oldest, the Norment-Parry Inn, is furnished with European and American antiques. Breakfast is served on the veranda of the antebellum manor that houses three lavish Edwardian guest rooms.

DoubleTree Castle
$$ 216 rooms

8629 International Dr. 407-934-1000 or 800-952-2785. www.doubletreecastle.com.

The next best thing to Cinderella's castle, this towering pink and purple palace is wildly tricked out with bejeweled thrones and mosaics of kings, queens and jesters. Renaissance music adds to the motif. Even the swimming pool carries the medieval theme with its mythical-monster fountain. It's certainly over-the-top, but great fun, and fits in perfectly with its International Drive location.

Holiday Inn Sunspree
$$ 507 rooms

13351 State Rd. 535. 407-239-4500 or 800-366-6299. www.kidsuites.com.

Close to the Disney parks, this hotel goes after family travelers in a big way. Kids check in at their own reservations desk and get a bag of goodies; rooms have outlet covers and other child-proof features. "Kidsuites" include a separate playhouse/bedroom for the kids, with TV, VCR and video games, and a mini-kitchenette. Kids age 12 and under eat free, and there's a special "kids only" restaurant. All this, and free shuttles to the theme parks.

Pop Century Resort
$$ 5,760 rooms

Disney Institute, 1901 Buena Vista Dr., Lake Buena Vista. 407-824-3200. www.disneyworld.com.

This is the newest entry in Disney's value-priced hotel category (along with the All-Star Movie, Music, and Sports resorts). Pop icons from the "Legendary Years" of the 1910s to 40s, and the "Classic Years" of the 50s to the 90s are the theme here—think giant-sized yo-yos, Play-Doh containers and Big Wheels. Older kids like the arcade/game room and food court. Take the resort shuttle bus to the Disney parks.

Westgate Lake
$$ 340 suites

10000 Turkey Lake Rd. 407-345-0000 or 800-424-0708. www.westgateresorts.com.

This woodsy 97-acre lakefront property offers a welcome sense of escape, even though the Disney parks are only 3mi away. Guests stay in one- to four-bedroom villas that sleep up to 16—making this a great choice for extended families. Outdoor amenities include a swimming pool, a beach and water sports, hot tubs and more.

STAYING IN THE TAMPA BAY AREA

Luxury

Don CeSar Beach Resort and Spa $$$$$ 277 rooms

3400 Gulf Blvd., St. Petersburg Beach. 727-360-1881. www.doncesar.com.

This flamingo-pink sand castle—complete with turrets and bell towers—is a St. Petersburg area landmark. Carrara-marble fountains and Cuban-tile floors evoke the hotel's jazz-age heyday when F. Scott Fitzgerald was a regular. Elegantly designed in breezy Florida pastels and light woods, guest rooms overlook the Gulf of Mexico or Boca Ciega Bay. The tony **Maritana Grille ($$$$)** serves fresh seafood in a dining room lined with saltwater aquariums.

Renaissance Vinoy Resort $$$$$ 360 rooms

501 Fifth Ave. NE, St. Petersburg. 727-894-1000. www.renaissancehotels.com.

Babe Ruth was among the celebrities who wintered at this opulent pink Mediterranean Revival 1925 landmark, considered one of St. Pete's architectural jewels. Overlooking Tampa Bay downtown, the resort has been restored to its former glory: Note the lobby's quarry-tile floors, stenciled cypress beams and frescoed ceilings. Bedrooms are done in contemporary blond oak furnishings and muted colors. Amenities include golf, tennis, a marina and a full spa.

Moderate

Don Vicente de Ybor Historic Inn $$$ 16 rooms

1915 Republica de Cuba (9th Ave. at 14th St.), Ybor City. 813-241-4545. www.donvicenteinn.com.

Crystal chandeliers, gilded furnishings and velvet draperies have transformed a former health-care center into a glitzy urban escape within Ybor City's lively Latin Quarter. Spacious suites feature draped beds, guest robes and slippers plus a private balcony. First owned by cigar manufacturer Vicente Martinez Ybor, the two-story 1895 structure now includes a 100-seat restaurant and a cigar and martini bar.

Mansion House B&B and the Courtyard on Fifth $$$ 13 rooms

105 Fifth Ave. NE, St. Petersburg. 727-821-9391 or 800-274-7520. www.mansionbandb.com.

Cozy and casual, this property includes two historic homes and a carriage house. Fresh flowers and hand-painted furniture add flair to guest rooms, and robes and light snacks are cheerfully provided by friendly innkeepers. Morning brings peaches-and-cream French toast, fresh fruit, and specialty cereals.

Index

The following abbreviations may appear in this Index: NHS National Historic Site; NM National Monument; NMem National Memorial; NP National Park; NHP National Historical Park; NWR National Wildlife Refuge; SP State Park; SHS State Historic Site.

Index

Index

Photos Courtesy Of:

Gwen Cannon/MICHELIN: 70, 97, 98, 99, 100, 101, 110; La Nouba by Cirque du Soleil®: 60; ©Disney: Front & back covers, 3, 4, 6, 7, 8, 9, 22, 23, 25, 26, 27, 28, 29, 30, 31, 32, 33, 34, 35, 36, 37, 38, 55, 56, 60, 61, 77, 78, 80, 83, 87, 90, 112-113; ©Disney/Pixar: 59; Harvey's Bistro: 115; ©Brigitta L. House/MICHELIN: 4, 21, 67, 95, 96; Hyatt Regency Grand Cypress Resort: 121; Image DJ Corp.: 91; Kennedy Space Center: 92, 93; Lakeridge Winery: 75; ©Lego: Cover (small); ©Norman Nokleby: 68; Orlando/Orange County CVB: 4, 50, 60, 61, 62, 63, 64, 65, 66, 71, 72, 74, 75, 76, 79, 82, 84, 85, 86, 88; The Peabody Orlando: 5, 114, 120; Renaissance Orlando Resort: 121; Ripley's Believe It or Not: 81; ©Salvador Dalí Museum, Inc.: 102; SeaWorld: 9, 39, 40, 41, 42, 43, 44, 57; Splendido & Chef David Lee *(Toronto, ON)*: icon pp. 112-117; Tampa Bay CVB: 5, 7, 8, 89, 105, 106, 107, 109, 123; ©2003 Universal Orlando: Cover (small right), 7, 8, 18-19, 45, 46, 47, 48, 49, 50, 51, 52, 53, 58, 118-119; White Wolf Café: 116.

Inside Front Cover: Base Map ©Mapquest.com